INCREDIBLE STORIES
CHANGEMAKERS OF BHARAT

INCREDIBLE STORIES
CHANGEMAKERS OF BHARAT

Niraj Kumar (Editor)

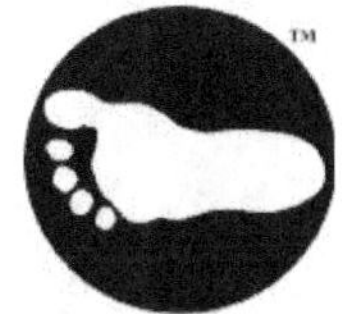

Bigfoot Publications
Because, there's a writer in everyone.

Incredible Stories: Changemakers of Bharat
Editor : Niraj Kumar

First Published by
Bigfoot06 Publications (OPC) Pvt. Ltd. B-10,12 Shree Shyam Palace, Sector 4,5 Chowk, Old Railway Road, Gurugram, Haryana (122001)
Website: www.bigfootpublications.in
Email: info@bigfootpublications.com

First Edition: November 2022
© Niraj Kumar

ISBN Print Book - **978-93-90925-89-6**

Printed in India

In Appreciation of the Book...

"Rarely one finds a book on the heroes of rural transformation. The book edited by Niraj Kumar is refreshing and interesting and a welcome addition to the existing literature on this hitherto ignored and less explored Subject...... *A must-read if you aspire to inspire.*"
The Daily Guardian

"An assortment of simple, straightforward, and inspiring stories which reads well—a commendable effort."
M. S. Sriram, Author and Visiting Professor, IIM Banglore

"This book uncovers the most critical aspects in the life of a changemaker - what happens when the romanticism of treading on an untrodden path gives way to the harsh realities of life; when one encounters the strong under-currents like social norms as one tries to initiate any change; when one is asked the tough questions, and how these exemplary heroes have dealt with those and have remained steadfastly committed to the cause that they chose to pursue."
Prabhat Labh, CEO, Grameen Foundation India

"There's nothing more satisfying than hearing the story of someone who has brought a positive social change around them. This book has not one but a dozen powerful inspirational stories about people who have done their part to make the world a better place, one corner at a time... can be read and re-read whenever one is looking for motivation."
Manju Menon, Cofounder and CEO, NuSocia

"A collection of profoundly compelling stories - explaining the impact of changemakers' gritty efforts on the lives they touched. Changes and disruptions for the better are needed and possible- these stories exemplify this. A valuable read for those interested in social transformation."
Sanjay Joshie, Executive Director, FES

"Alive stories of endless struggle, courage, and perseverance against all odds. Reading about how women members of Nirvaya fought for their rights, how tribal farmers reorganised to rejuvenate mulberry sericulture, or about women's self-help groups that brought the solar lighting revolution to villages will fill one with hope and inspiration and, above all, ignite a spark to become a changemaker."
Seyed Faiz, Program Manager, OXFAM UK

"Exciting, real, and enlightening. By reading this collection of stories, even a novice can apprehend the villages' simplicity and complexities, the villagers' naivety and astuteness and most important- the exemplary heroism of local leaders. Kudos to the authors."
Sanjeev Kapoor, Professor, IIM Lucknow

"Real and gripping.... Sometimes young people struggle to find their purpose and calling. This compendium of fascinating stories of ordinary people with extraordinary impact will certainly inspire the readers to find the true value of their lives."
Paromita Goswami, Professor, Shiv Nadar University, Noida

Contents

Foreword

I draw much satisfaction from my lifelong association with the rural people of India, Bharat. As a member of the founding team of PRADAN in the 1980's, and through SRIJAN, the civil society organisation I founded in 1997, and now through the Buddha Fellowship Program of the Buddha Institute, I have been fortunate to have played a part in positively impacting millions of poor at the bottom of the social pyramid in India. I know for sure that doing so is probably one of the most challenging missions one can undertake in life. One needs to surrender the comforts and the personal aspirations one could have for oneself or for one's family.

Prof. Niraj Kumar, the editor of the book, has been my old friend. I accept that I hardly had any opportunity to work closely with him, but his professional credentials as an academic and an expert on the subject of this book are well-established. Further, he is known for his storytelling and case-writing skills. In addition, many of the co-authors are associated with PRADAN, the organisation where I first learned the basics of development. Hence when Niraj approached me with a request to write a foreword for this book which tells the stories of heroes of rural transformation, I was delighted to accept the offer.

Based on my experience and exposure, I can say that the literary and academic world, at least in India, has been a bit economical with writing and publishing the contribution of the development sector in nation-building. We in RCRC, the coalition of over 90 civil society organisations with an outreach of 1.6 crore Indians in 110 districts, realise that there are only a few attempts to document the life stories of unsung heroes who have devoted their lives to uplifting the poor. Dhruvi Shah and I tried to fill the gap by publishing The Book of Aspiration – a collection of memoirs of ten carefully selected social leaders. I am glad this book by Niraj and his co-authors goes much further and deeper.

After going through the manuscript, I can confidently say that the editor and his co-authors have made a valiant attempt to reverse the trend. Besides a well-crafted agenda-setting prologue, the book carries twelve stories of field-based changemakers and community leaders' journeys from sufferings to happiness. Just to illustrate, Sailabala was able to secure land rights for single women in the Rayagada district! Although different authors have written the stories, uniformity in the format and presentation of stories makes reading much easier. There is a greater focus on women-led stories, which is commendable.

The book identifies some of the most critical socio-economic issues, such as land rights for women. These have haunted our rural areas for decades and are responsible for continuing suffering of people living there. Besides the government, various civil society organisations in India have done commendable jobs addressing these issues. Of late Indian corporations (through their CSR works) also have joined the bandwagon. But these are the dedicated volunteers and development professionals – the true changemakers working in challenging conditions, who actually make it possible on the ground. The book tells the stories of twelve such selected changemakers.

The uniqueness of the book doesn't lie in the challenges but in the innovative strategies the changemakers have adopted and the ingenuity with which they executed them. As each story progresses along a series of problems and solutions, optimism and frustration, failure and success, the reader will easily relate to and identify with the contexts and characters. The narrations are so natural that you will find yourself submerged in the realities of rural India, i.e., Bharat. I am sure, like me, the reader should find the book engaging and inspiring.

With best wishes to Niraj and his team.

Ved Arya

Founder – SRIJAN, and The Buddha Institute
National Convenor- RCRC
Hubert H Humphrey North-South Fellow
Ashoka Fellow; Aspire Fellow

Acknowledgements

First, the changemakers and the community whose stories we have covered in this book deserve our foremost and earnest acknowledgement, and I record it with all sincerity.

I would like to express my most sincere gratitude to my co-authors, who remained steadfast in their conviction to share accurate and 'live from the field' stories despite the pandemic that raged across the country, creating havoc. Their conviction and readiness to share the stories of their communities have made the book possible. They readily submitted to my continued badgering over deadlines and repeated requests to re-write the stories, although they had enough other commitments of their own.

The team PRADAN proved an excellent collaborator and facilitator. I could experience the value and dedication that have been the hallmark of every PRADANite whenever I interacted with them. However, I cannot stop myself from making a special mention of Manas Satpathy of PRADAN, to whom I first broached the idea of writing these case stories and sought his help. His instant positive response was not only heartening but also reassuring, and he stood by me throughout my journey. My heartfelt gratitude.

My sincere thanks to Fr. Antony R. Uvari, SJ. And Fr. S. Antony Raj, Vice-Chancellor and Registrar, respectively, of XIM University, Bhubaneswar, who were unstinting in their encouragement and support.

Anxiety is normal for the first-time author or editor of any book. However, after talking to Deepak Yadav of BigFoot Publications, I was not only relieved but was also sure that my manuscript was going to be handled by a team of professionals dedicated to their craft. I express my profound appreciation for Deepak Ji and his team.

But for Yateendra Joshi, this book would not have been so neat and composed. He has been so meticulous in his what I call 'editing-plus' work that we did not have to go through the manuscripts once he had okayed them.

For me, writing or editing is mostly a solitary affair. Had it not been for my wife, Priya, I would not have been able to perform the task to the best of my capacity. As she has been doing for almost three decades, she fed me to keep my body and soul strong enough that I could be fit and face emotional highs and lows. I remain grateful to her forever.

My daughter, Jayati, reads all my writing and comments on them with an expert's enthusiasm, claiming that she has been a Loyolean and a Sophian. Her suggestions did help me in improving my writing. The magnanimous appreciation of my academic achievements by my younger brother, Amit, and his wife, Priti have always been a morale booster for me. Thanks a lot, all of you.

The unstinting help received from Dibyakshi Khale, one of my favourite students, has been heartening. My heartfelt blessings to her.

As I recapitulate my professional journey, I realise that many of my friends and fellow students at GBPUAT and IVRI and colleagues from IIFM, XIMB, DMI, IIML, and XIM University have influenced me for the better. To each one of those individuals, I remain obligated.

I thank Mr Anil Kr. Badajena, my colleague at the School of Rural Management office for all the assistance I needed during the book writing period.

And finally, I bow to my parents and the Almighty for granting me everything I needed to complete this book.

Niraj Kumar

Let's Start...
(Niraj Kumar)

PRELUDE

Breaking News: Padma Awardees for 2021 declared! I remember watching the news channels with much excitement, to know the names of the award winners. Several names were well known, but few of them were unheard. I got to know about these new names after a Google search. They are all ordinary people with extraordinary accomplishments. Working in nondescript corners of the country and away from the media glare, these people have changed the lives of many with their hard work, dedication, and perseverance. These ordinary people are the real heroes and change makers of our country.

Many of the Indian youth today are yearning to be a part of and contribute to the changes the Indian hinterland is undergoing. They are intelligent, tech-savvy risk-takers, sensitive to social and environmental issues, and ready to walk down the muddy road in the scorching heat, if it brings smiles to the faces of common people and make mother earth a better place for living. They need convincing answers to a few of their questions.

There are two sets of nagging questions in the minds of Indian youth, especially the urban youth. The first set comprises questions such as: What is the Indian hinterland really like? Why are people who live there poor? What do NGOs do in villages? How does change come about in rural areas? Are villagers wary of outsiders and reluctant to embrace change?

The second set contains questions such as: How can an ordinary person bring about a significant change? Can villagers themselves be the drivers of their transformation? How can I become the next Waterman of India (Rajendra Singh), the next Chipko leader (Sundar Lal Bahuguna), Baba Amte, or Kailash Satyarthi in the days to come? How can I be one of the true champions and change makers of rural India or Bharat? Will my decisions for social change prove to be wise ones in the future?

The above questions are natural and only to be expected. It is a testimony to changing India that more and more people, particularly the younger ones are asking these questions. They deserve authentic answers from those with first-hand experience. Unfortunately, all they get is armchair theories, mountains of data, glib solutions slickly explained or half-true stories presented as either romantic or pathetic.

The twelve hard-hitting stories in this book tell us what the hinterland is really like and how villagers struggle with and triumph over seemingly insurmountable challenges. These true stories narrate sagas of pain and suffering, awakening and action, of grassroots leadership and teamwork. They bear witness to how ordinary men and women in Indian villages have shaped the lives and destinies of millions. These are the inspirational stories of those unsung champions, who have positively transformed the lives of thousands in nondescript corners of the country.

The characters and contexts of these unsung tales of adventure make it evident that one does not always need enormous resources to make a difference. Instead, one needs empathy, faith in the power of collectives, innovative thinking, and the ability to influence and empower the community. The heroes of our stories believe in a philosophy of empowerment rather than paternalism, in partnerships rather than benefactor-beneficiary relationships, and processes rather than outcomes of actions. Their success criteria include happy people, better incomes, improved lives, and a sustainable environment. Though all these seem idealistic and hard to achieve in real life, the true stories in this book will prove otherwise.

The stories, which are shortlisted exclusively for this book, are drawn from the hundreds of successful interventions of Pradan, one of India's internationally acclaimed NGOs. Since its inception in 1983, Pradan has been able to change the lives of millions of Indians, especially women across the country. In recognition of the contribution of Pradan, its co-founder Mr Deep Joshi was awarded the 2009 Ramon Magsaysay Award for bringing professionalism to the NGO movement in India.

Co-authored by grassroots professionals and practising academicians, these stories take readers along the journey from pain to contentment, transporting them to villages in the hinterland to experience what life is really like: to see parched fields turned into green pastures, single and destitute women taking charge of their lands to become a source of inspiration, corrupt and lethargic village councils being revitalized to become agents of change . . . These extraordinary stories of ordinary people living in remote villages will electrify readers of all ages and from any walk of life, especially those who are committed to change India's villages and making them powerhouses of India's forward march.

Although every story is different — with varied situations, challenges and players — they have the same message: be innovative, take the community along in overcoming obstacles, and make lives better for everyone. They reiterate that you need not be superhuman to bring positive change. As each story progresses along a chain of setbacks and solutions, of hope and despair, defeats and victories, readers will relate to and identify with the settings and characters. I am sure they will never ever want to leave the story halfway and will cherish their journey to the final triumph.

For every hero in this book, there are many others who have already made their mark and many others who are still arduously working for change. This book will give them gratification, renewed hope, and strength.

This unique experiment of collaboration between field professionals and academicians has yielded exceptional results. Each story has been co-authored by a field professional and a researcher. Hence, the stories are real, and the narrations are inspirational. It is possible that your 'rational and temporal' mind might look at our stories as just stories and tell you to ignore them. But, it is also possible that your 'sensitive and humane' heart will urge you to learn from these stories and do something for the better. This book will undoubtedly prove to be a catalyst for those thinking of doing something different, and aspiring to be amongst the country's heroes.

Everyone desires to be a champion of change, a messiah of the poor, and a saviour of nature. I sincerely hope the enriching stories in this book will trigger you into positive action.

*****

The Pain and Joy of Women's Empowerment

(Gautam Prateek & Sailabala Panda)

"We are members of the Nirvaya federation and have come to take the girl back with us. If your tradition requires negotiations before getting the girl married… However,return The girl to us first."

The story begins...

On 1 September 2016, Bandhaguda, a village in the Kolnara block of Rayagada district of Odisha, witnessed a sixteen-year-old girl's abduction by her maternal cousins. The minor girl was held hostage in Wardha, another village, quite far from where the she lived. Although few of the villagers defended abduction as part of the social norms that allowed young and unmarried girls to be abducted for marriage, the event left the villagers, particularly women, in deep shock.

It took a few hours for the village to come to terms with the untoward incident and to start talking about it. When the news of the abduction reached *Nirvaya*, an all-women federation in the district fighting for women's rights, its members held an urgent meeting and decided to work for the immediate release of the abducted girl. It was no coincidence that just a day earlier, the girl's mother had participated in the formal registration of Nirvaya. However, the organisation had begun working for women's rights in the Kolnara block two years ago. And only hours later, she was undergoing what now seemed like a test of grit and resolve. Sailabala Panda from *Pradan*, and one of the founding members of *Nirvaya*, claimed: "Although the abduction was being defended on the pretext that it was a social norm, the real reason was the unsettled debt of 1000 rupees incurred by the girl's father."

Travelling in a hired Maruti van, four members of *Nirvaya*, under the leadership of Sailabala, managed to reach Wardha in the middle of the night. The villagers had been expecting someone from Bandhaguda to negotiate the girl's return. On being confronted by the all- women team of negotiators, elders from Wardha requested the team to return and insisted that some elders from Bandhaguda be the negotiators instead. Durga Ram, a man with a thick moustache, said, "This is as per our community's age-old traditions and customs; no wrong has been committed, and the girl is safe. Please send someone more mature from your village for discussions."

Sailabala said, "We are members of the *Nirvaya* federation, and we have come to take the girl back with us. If your tradition requires negotiations before getting the girl married, we will inform our village elders accordingly and request them to visit Wardha. However, return the girl to us first."

"What is this *Nirvaya* federation? Are they superior to our community? Even the police don't interfere with our community and culture. We will not hand over the girl to you without negotiations", declared one Durgaram, with apparent anger.

It was midnight, and more than 100 villagers had surrounded the van, parked almost at the centre of Wardha. As time went by, people began to whisper; the whispers soon became murmurs, and, as the numbers soared, the murmurs turned to a commotion. Yet team *Nirvaya* remained resolute and started talking to a couple of older women who were part of the crowd instead of remaining silent. It was more than two hours since team *Nirvaya* had reached Wardha, but there was no sign of any solution. Despite the evident hostility and tension, the members of Nirvaya were adamant that they wouldn't leave without the girl.

The crowd began to split into smaller groups. Although the commotion had subsided to some extent, the hubbub grew louder. Women, too, were found discussing animatedly among themselves. The van and *Nirvaya* members remained encircled by the villagers, mainly children.

Suddenly, the circle opened at a point, and everyone began looking toward the point of the breach. A girl, escorted by two men and two women, was advancing slowly towards the car. The girl looked pale and exhausted, and her face and eyes were swollen. She ran towards the van as soon as she spotted Sailabala and others from her village. All the Nirvaya members ran towards the girl, hugged her, and held her tight. Then, the girl started sobbing loudly. However, Sailabala and her team got the girl into the car without wasting time. Within five minutes, Sailabala was back in the car after exchanging some hurried words of parting with a few older women. The car gathered speed in no time – the abduction ended as dawn broke.

A village girl is abducted, a group of fearless young women from her village reach the village she was being held captived, and, within a few hours, the girl is back home – with no help from the law, no ransom, no scuffle – reunited with her family. The sequence looks more like a well-executed film script. But questions such as how *Nirvaya* came into existence and how its members managed to be so fearless remain unanswered.

"Although the reasons behind *Nirvaya*'s birth and existence are not unique to India, they have to do with unequal rights of men and women in our society. This all-women federation came into existence to fight for and claim women's natural and constitutional rights", explained Sailabala, who is regarded as the main force behind *Nirvaya*. After a small pause, she continued, "You know, Rayagada is a predominantly tribal district with 56% of its total population being tribal, and the Kondhs with whom we work constitute a little over 70% of the total tribal population. Our women sisters participate in most farming activities and understand local farming practices but own only a fraction of operational landholdings. They lack legal title or ownership and are deemed ineligible for credit and government welfare schemes. A combination of legal, sociocultural, and economic factors makes a single woman's access to land in this district particularly precarious."

"Sir, may I add a few more points related to the district in which we are working?" asked Sabitri, a young member of *Nirvaya* who was regarded as a firebrand activist in the region. Even before anybody could respond, she continued: "our organization *Pradan*, conducted research in twelve villages in two administrative blocks of the district to know the status of women. The findings were an eye-opener. Of the 250 households surveyed, single women constituted 34% of the total respondents. Among the single women, 19% were widows, and 14% had never married –and all were poor."

Offering a perfunctory apology for throwing all these numbers at us, Sabitri went on in her distinct style to highlight the plight of women in the district: "Thirty-nine percent of the households, including those headed by single women, are landless. Lack of access to land makes life miserable for single women. They may be unmarried daughters, widows, or married but deserted by their husbands." Sabitri took a deep breath and continued, "Sir, we were lucky that *Pradan* took the initiative and decided to form a block-level organisation.

May God bless Sailabala *didi*; we now have an active institution", Sabitri added as she ended her long but informative monologue.

These women appeared different. They were well aware of their rights and believed that mere begging for or simply demanding the rights would achieve nothing. They were ready to fight. Further inquiries revealed that *Nirvaya* resulted from the sustained effort put in by team *Pradan* to bring women together, from forming self-help groups at the village level to a federation of the groups at the block level *Nirvaya*. "My objective was to ensure that women had equal rights in society and were given land rights to minimise their suffering. Single women, in particular, were in dire need of land rights", recalled Sailabala.

However, men in the villages didn't seem happy about the organisation, which, in their opinion, was changing the social norms and the village culture. Gender disparities, according to them, were part of the social tradition. As a village elder whose daughter had been abandoned by her husband put it, "If we give land to our daughters, it becomes part of their in-laws' property." This remark summed up the prevalent thinking.

"I am not surprised that even government officials were reluctant to appreciate single women's land rights demand", said Sabitri.

A circular from the Department of Revenue and Disaster Management, Government of Odisha, on the enumeration of landlessness (the Vasundhara scheme launched in 2015 by the Odisha government) raised the hopes of the members of *Nirvaya*, who regarded the scheme as the means to achieve their objectives. The members called on the village level revenue officer (*tehsildar*) to express their willingness to participate in the scheme and suggested a workshop held jointly by *Nirvaya* and the department to explain the newly launched scheme.

The request was granted, and the workshop was organised.

Besides the village revenue officer and members of *Nirvaya*, the revenue supervisor, the revenue inspector, and other officials of the revenue circle also participated in the workshop and contributed to developing formats for the enumeration of households that owned no land or even a homestead. In addition, *Nirvaya*, in consultation with the tehsildar, identified a few local women and trained them to be enumerators.

Nirvaya wanted to identify single women separately, but the tehsildar's views differed. He spelt out his concern: "Single women should not be identified as eligible for the scheme ... their inclusion will send a wrong message to society.... More and more women will want to be separated from their husbands for the land's sake." "This attitude shocked us, but we had anticipated such reactions; we continued to persuade the tehsildar and other senior officials and prevailed on them until they agreed that the proposed survey, or enumeration, will also identify single women", recalled a contented Sabitri.

The enumeration was completed within a month and covered 75 revenue villages. In each village, special *palli sabhas* (meetings of village-level institutions) were organised in the presence of panchayat (village council) representatives. A total of 1946 homesteads had women as their heads, of which 660 were single women. As the families enumerated were more than the revenue department's annual target for providing land titles, 453 households were given land titles, of which single women headed 60.

This was like the second and absolute independence for the women of our village. "Until yesterday, the rights of lands were only for men. Land in the name of women has now become a reality. We understand how crucial this was for us. Now, we feel women are equal to men in every sphere", Mami Pedantis, an active member of *Nirvaya*, explained the excitement over their life-changing achievement.

This, no doubt, had boosted the federation's confidence and of women members in collective power. However, the question - how they could become so courageous and achieve so much in such little time - continued to weigh on my mind. I decided to ask Sailabala herself.

A smiling Sailabala explained, "It was not something unique; we followed the simple process of making key stakeholders, including the women, youth and men in the Kondh community, and government officials, aware of the problems women face in villages. We trained village women to register and process the claim of members' rights to forests and homesteads."

Seeing my interest in knowing the story of the rise of women fighters, Sailabala continued with added zest, "Parallel to this work we continued to develope trust in the group, strengthening members' self-confidence, and exploring livelihood options through the convergence of other schemes linked to land use. Our sisters were trained to raise the issue of women's land rights emphatically and vociferously on every platform."

Introducing a woman member standing next to her, Sailabala said, "*Bhaiya, kam to bahut karna pada lekin ab parinaam aata hai to achha lagta hai. Ye dekho, Jiyamma behan izzat se hans kar jee rahi hai. Ye sab aisi bahno ki ladai ka phal hai.* (Brother, we had to work very hard, but now, it gives us satisfaction when we get positive results. My fellow sisters are living with pride, and all this is the result of their fight). Taking up women's issues, for example, those of Jiyammma's and Sabitri's, kept the group focused, united, and active in the fight for the core issues. Stories of our sisters will help you better understand what we are." Sailabala then requested Jiyamma, a woman in her 40s, to narrate the story of her suffering and liberation.

We decided to take a break. Hemvati, from *Pradan*, served tea to everyone. As Jiyamma waited for her tea to reach a comfortable temperature, Hemvati began her story. She got married when she was only 15. Her parents had to sell their land to get her married. For the first two years of marriage, all was well" ... "*Nahi, Sir; ek saal ke baad se hi usne maar-pitai shuru kar diya*" (No, Sir; within a year, he started beating me), interrupted Jiyamma.

Hemvati then asked Jiyamma to take up the story herself. "Even before my son was born, my husband had started beating me, and no one from his family ever attempted to protect me. For the first 6 months, I didn't share this with anyone, but later on, I started resisting and sharing my problems with some women from the village. Some older women even tried to counsel him, but he did not mend his ways. He would go away and not return for days together. He had dumped me. I would go hungry for days, but neither he nor his family members would ask after me. The last straw was when he returned accompanied by a woman from a nearby village, whom he declared to be his wife, and asked me to get lost. I fought, but with help from other family members, he threw me out of his house. I appealed to members of the self-help group to which I belonged, but they could not do much. My little son, too, was taken away from me." The memory reduced her to tears, and she could not continue.

Seeing Jiyamma weeping, Hemvati began speaking again. "Those were the early days of *Nirvaya* when Jiyamma joined us. The federation helped her get all the basic documents such as an *aadhar* card (a proof of identity issued by the Central government and used across the country) and a ration card (entitles one to get rice, wheat, sugar, etc. at subsidised rates). Jiyamma was enrolled in the panchayat office as a single woman with no property. Although she started getting a form of aid from the government, she also began working as a labourer on daily wages to survive. From the day she joined, she was among the most active members of our federation. She could relate to the sufferings of other members and identify herself with most of the federation's objectives. She was among the first beneficiaries who got a land *patta* (title deed or lease) for a plot about 1685 square metres (40 decimals, a decimal being one-hundredth of an acre or 435.6 square feet) from the government. As a result of her hard work, she is not only financially independent but helps her son, who has been reunited with her. She now lives with her head held high", concluded Hemvati. All I could say was a 'Wow'!

Nirvaya was already a success story. Women of this tribal district of Odisha had shown that women were no longer the weaker sex; instead, they were now strong enough to change the decades-old social norms and to challenge the working of the organs of the

State.

Buoyed by the success of guaranteeing the rights of single women to homestead land, *Nirvaya* began extending its efforts in 2018 towards ensuring women's rights to forest land, using the Forest Rights Act, 2006 (which recognizes the rights of the forest-dwelling tribal communities and other traditional forest dwellers to forest resources). Although it did not take much time and effort, winning the rights to the forest for women was another feather in the cap of *Nirvaya* and a watershed in the history of women empowerment in Odisha. The story of Sabitri Hikaka tells it all.

Sabitri Hikaka, a single woman in Boriguda, had lost her parents at a young age and had to shoulder the responsibility of her 3 younger siblings. Sabitri's uncles had refused to share the ancestral property with Sabitri because she was a girl. She worked hard to make ends meet and remained unmarried to support her family. After some training related to the Forest Rights Act, a forest rights committee was formed in the village, and Sabitri was selected as its president. A total of 75 households in the village have been able to claim their rights as individuals, and 21 of the claimants were single women.

"Continued engagement with all the villagers – men and women, and with government officials helped the *palli sabha* and the forest department to entertain the claim of those single women", explained Sailabala, and went on to further add, "In fact, in the process, the members of the forest rights committee even approached local politicians to garner support for their claims. After receiving the title to two acres of land, Sabitri began cultivating vegetables and rice. She is a member of a village-producer group and is also linked to the block-level women farmers' organization. As a result, she receives better-quality inputs (such as seeds and fertilizers) and support for marketing her farm produce. Today, Sabitri is both a role model and an inspiration to other vulnerable women in the entire area. Land rights for single women have proved crucial to their well-being and have made them respectable members of society". Proud Sailabala sounded both contended and proud.

Afterword

Building on the success stories of Rayagada, the project on women's rights to land has now been upscaled to 4000 villages spread across 3 states, namely Odisha, Chhattisgarh, and Jharkhand. Recognizing her exemplary contributions, Sailabala Panda has been given the responsibility of leading the project in all three states. Today, Sailabala is a known face among the tribal community of the Rayagada district and is considered an activist and a saviour of poor and vulnerable women. When asked how it feels to know that hundreds of women are better off and empowered because of her leadership, she replied, "It is all because of my sisters in the villages and our organization, *Pradan*; I am merely a conduit, a means to an end."

Chasi Bandhus: The Life Changers

(Balram Bhushan & Sourav Maity)

"For these villagers, empowerment is not about earning money but about creating a dignified identity for self, sharing equal responsibilities in the family, and, most importantly, having a say in family and village decision-making."

The story begins...

Travelling in a long-distance bus after the second wave of the Covid 19 pandemic was no less than an adventure, especially in one full of foodies and politically well-aware people. Yes, I was travelling to West Bengal from Odisha. My fellow travellers left no stone unturned to defy the fear of Corona. I was thrilled to see their enthusiasm for sharing their food and thoughts. Suddenly, a passenger started a political debate, saying, "India is a country of large numbers. A leader can become a chief minister or even a prime minister by winning as little as 30-35% of the votes. No one cares about the real majority, those 65-70% who oppose the same person."

Another passenger sitting next to me said, "Polity reflects society. Do we really care about the majority of our population? They live in rural India. Hence, we ignore them. Their occupation is agriculture, and hence we ignore farmers; women are silent workers and work for 24 hours, and we ignore them. If you want to change polity, change the society first."

Then a third one jumped in from the last row of seats, "There is no hope for the villagers, farmers, and the women in India. Why will the elite relinquish their power and help them?"

A young traveller, quietly listening to this discussion, politely said, "It is not about helping them but letting them help themselves. We need to give them opportunities and guide them, and they will emerge empowered. We work around these challenges—women empowerment through agriculture and rural development. The idea is straightforward: bring the 50% of the ignored village population, i.e., women, into economic activities to develop the community as a whole."

Listening to this discussion, I found the topic for my next story, namely 'Meeting of two infinities: women empowerment through agriculture'. After an hour, the bus stopped for refreshments. I approached the man who had spoken of his work on the empowerment of women. I expressed my interest in knowing more about his works and his ideas on the subject.

I said to him, "People like you are real gems. When most people fail to see even the day-to-day challenges that women face, you are talking about empowering women. It challenges the existing social order, which means you must be facing a lot of opposition. How do you manage this heroic task? "

He replied, "I represent *Pradan* ; as an organisation, we do nothing except being a part of rural women's successes and failures. We simply add the spark, but they follow their own trajectory of empowerment and, in doing so, add value to their family and the community."

I asked, "Spark!? What is that?"

"Spark is the realisation of their strength", he replied, and then added: "We train them in modern farming methods and add to their dignity and respect by calling them '*Chasi Bandhus*' (farmer's friend). We intervene at two levels: we add to their strengths and make them aware of them. If they know who they are, they will communicate that knowledge to the rest of the world."

"What is '*Chasi Bandhu*'? Explain it for me," I politely requested.

"Let me first introduce myself; I am Saurabh, and I work for an organisation called *Pradan*. To learn about '*Chasi Bandhu*,' you must see who they are and what they do. And for that, you should come with me to Lalgarh and experience their life first-hand."

I had heard a lot about *Pradan*, and without second thoughts, I promised him that I'd visit Lalgarh the following Sunday.

I reached Lalgarh and found Saurabh waiting for me. "Welcome, Sir," he said, "We will visit a village that, to my knowledge, has never seen any development efforts." He shared a few printed pages with me as we headed towards the village. Those pages had some details about the block (an administrative unit) in which Saurabh had been promoting '*Chasi Bandhus*'.

The block comprised 543 villages with a total population of about 1.58 lakh. More than 52% were from the Scheduled Castes and Scheduled Tribes, which are among the oppressed communities chosen for affirmative action by India's Constitution. The list of such communities is part of a schedule of the Constitution, hence the label 'Scheduled'. Although more than 62% of the block's population was literate, more than 53% of the women were illiterate.

'*Chasi Bandhu*' has been an evolving idea. After *Pradan* arrived in Lalgarh, Saurabh and his team began working with self-help groups (SHGs). Initial discussions with local women made them realise that they were not only hard-working but also enterprising, and their village lay in one of the fertile areas of the state. Unfortunately, development had passed the village by. Although a good number of development schemes had been introduced by the Central government and the State government for the benefit of the people, neither the villagers were aware of those schemes nor had the concerned government departments taken any initiatives to reach these villagers. After Saurabh gave some background information, we discussed the self-help groups and team *Pradan*.

Saurabh planned to turn some women into development professionals. Although he was aware that many women in the village had leadership qualities and could be the right fit for becoming village-level development professionals, their selection was going to be a tricky process. Saurabh didn't want to impose his preferences on them but, at the same time, didn't want to choose only those who were popular choices if that meant compromising efficiency and competency. So, he explained what he needed and requested local village groups to nominate those they considered most suitable for the job. For Saurabh and his team, except for convincing the family members of the nominated members, overall nomination and bringing the chosen candidates on board proved easy.

"What were the objections of family members?" I asked.

Saurabh replied, "Families believed these women would be required to give more time to the village and to social work and, consequently, their household chores would suffer. Also, husbands and elders in the family were sceptical of sending their women members for such 'outside' work."

Training the nominated leaders involved a great deal of effort, but the women were quite forthcoming and keen to learn. They felt empowered when they realised that they would be 'Chasi Bandhus', who would decide the direction and fate of farming in their village. Today, 41 'chashi bandhus' work in six villages, advising villagers on livelihood, farming, and fisheries. The 'Chasi Bandhus' help farmers access state-run schemes such as *Kisaan Credit Card* (bank credit to farmers at low interest), *Krishak Bandhu* (half-yearly financial support to farmers), *Pradhan Mantri Krishi Samman Nidhi* (annual financial support to farmers), *Motsyojibi Credit Card* (bank credit at low interest for fisheries), *Bangla Fasal Bima* (crop insurance scheme), and one-time assistance for (buying) small farm implements (OTA-SFI). As a result, farmers learned more about modern farming methods and were able to get higher yields. In addition, farmers became more aware of the concerns related to the use of agro-chemicals. The villagers now had access to technologies and schemes they had not known about before.

All this left me deeply impressed. "Unbelievable!" I said, "How can these illiterate and semi-literate women do so much? How did you make all these possible?"

Saurabh burst into a peal of laughter. He said, "Sir, I knew you'd ask this – a question that tops my list of FAQs (frequently asked questions)." He answered, "most of the credit for this transformation should go to these women who decided to come forward to contribute. The initial training and handholding did help, but the convergence of government schemes and support from the State agriculture department and the MGNREGA (a Central-government- run employment guarantee scheme) has been continuous and substantial. Now, these women visit the relevant offices at the block level and demand the implementation of government schemes".

We had reached Lalgarh by the time and were welcomed by seven women. Saurabh introduced me and said, "Here are the real '*Chasi Bandhus*'. You talk to them, find out who are they and what they do, and learn from them."

One of them spoke before I could get a word in: "Dada, '*Chasi Bandhu*' is a woman who takes care of her family, community, and village. We are everywhere: in MGNREGA work, farming, and marketing farm produce. We are housewives, but we are proud to be working housewives."

I asked, "Working housewives? What is that? How is your day different from that of a typical housewife and that of a typical working woman if you call yourself a working housewife?"

Thakurmani Hansda, in her 40s, a *'Chasi Bandhu'* herself, described her typical day, "We usually wake up at four in the morning. After cooking for our family and completing other household chores, we reach the meeting point by about 7 o'clock, a spot to which many farmers bring their harvest of vegetables for grading, sorting, and packing. We help them sell the produce to commission agents or traders at reasonable prices and close to the market rate. On returning home in the afternoon, we tend to our cattle and then visit our fields to take care of our crops. In the evening, we call on our farmer friends to know more about issues related to farming. After that, we cook and dine, update our diary and papers, and plan for the next day before turning in."

I asked Saurabh, "What about women empowerment? They are working 24x7 and seem to have become workaholics."

Saurabh shook his head and said, "Oh, this fancy corporate jargon. If you really want to know whether they are driven by compulsion or choice, let me introduce you to Mousumi Patra. Ask her whether she feels helpless or empowered. Listen to her story." He then turned to a woman trying to follow our conversation and make sense of it.

"Becoming a *'Chasi Bandhu'* has changed my entire family's life. Today I own a scooty (a small two-wheeler), which I bought out of what I earned by training members of self-help groups. Now I own and use a new smartphone as well. Sir, recently I underwent an operation to remove a gallbladder stone, and I could pay Rs 20,000/- from my savings, out of a total of Rs 30,000/- for the treatment. Now I help my family members and pay for my children's education. Every official of the Gram Panchayat and the block office and local political leaders recognise me by name, and I get due recognition in my village because of my work", Mousumi shared her story in one go.

Saurabh added, "For these villagers, empowerment is not about earning money but about creating a dignified identity for self, sharing equal responsibilities in the family, and, most importantly, having a say in family and village decision-making."

Mousumi's face clearly showed her feelings. On the one hand, she explained her pains and struggles before she started working as a '*Chasi Bandhu*'; on the other, she was proud of her courage and achievements. After listening to her for some time, I said, "Yes, your life has really changed. Carry on your good work."

It was then Thakurmani's turn to speak. She thought she had been fortunate to become a '*Chasi Bandhu*'. She said, "My husband and my brother-in-law supported me a lot after I decided to become a '*Chasi Bandhu*'. They convinced me that it is a service that needs my interest and patience. Farming is a vast sector, and farming technologies continue to develop rapidly. Although I can't read and write Bengali efficiently, my family members read different reading materials provided to me during my '*Chasi Bandhu*' training and helped me understand their contents. Now, I can work independently."

As the discussion continued and became even more animated, we decided to sit down under a tree. Phulmani, yet another '*Chasi Bandhu*', said, "Dada, not everybody is lucky to have a husband, in-laws, and people around who are good and encourage women members to work outside the home. Sometimes even simple and useful suggestions are not welcome. Take my example: when I ventured to suggest to my husband that we should try out SRI, the system for rice intensification, on 1 bigha of land (about 1700 square metres), he became angry and replied rudely that it was his land and not my father's; that I was only expected to transplant paddy seedlings when asked to do so; that I should remember my place as a mere helper and not make decisions related to farming." When I persisted, he said, "you can try out the SRI over half the area, but if you fail, you would have to work as a labourer on somebody else's farm to make up for the loss."

"I felt humiliated and understood my status in my family. I was further embarrassed that I had been reprimanded in front of my daughter-in-law. However, I did not gave up and continued to work as '*Chasi Bandhu*'. I succeeded, and now I feel empowered. I have money to spend; my husband no longer drinks and is no longer violent, and my family supports me. I feel confident because I am in charge of my life and make my own decisions," recounted Phulmani.

Mousumi Patra took up the thread once again and recalled her experience. "Initially, people would question '*Chasi Bandhus*' like me and our knowledge of farming, which they considered as a man's work. Men believe that they don't need to learn anything from a woman . . . Even my family challenged me to prove what I had learnt as a '*Chasi Bandhu*' by growing vegetables on a small piece of land. I accepted the challenge and grew vegetables over 10 'decimals' (one-tenth of an acre, or roughly 400 square metres). I did everything from putting up trellises to support the vines, ploughing, sowing, weeding, buying and applying bio-fertilizers, spraying to control pests, and harvesting. I made a profit of Rs 9000. Then, in the same plot, I grew green grams in summer. Nobody thought green gram could be grown on our land. I have been the first to adopt many new crops and methods. Now my fellow farmers, both men and women, turn to me for advice on what they should grow. Although the pandemic meant reduced income for many, including farmers, that is not the case here. Now farmers are respectful to me whenever I visit them and actively listen to my suggestions. I am a proud '*Chasi Bandhu*'."

Monika, a widow, living in Lalgarh with her mother, happily worked as '*Chasi Bandhu*'. However, unfortunately, her mother compelled her to work as a maid servant in the house of a rich doctor in a nearby town. Monika resisted but couldn't say no to her mother. After all, the family needed more money to take care of Monika's two young daughters.

Afterword

I decide to go around Lalgarh. Although the farms were smaller, they were irrigated and were lush green with standing crops. Both men and women worked in the fields. "Where are their children?", I asked.

"In school", was Saurabh's terse answer. He continued, "Sir, most of the members started hoping that this work would improve their lot and reduce their suffering. Soon, it dawned on them that it was a win-win game and that they would earn money, respect and dignity, which had eluded them for generations. Now children of all 'Chasi Bandhus' attend school; a few of them even have a college degree and have started working. Migration for work to nearby places has almost stopped. The average income of villagers has gone up by 70%. They grow more crops, sell the produce locally, and make a profit."

I remembered what Kanaklata, another 'Chasi Bandhu', had told me: "Now, we are better off than before. We work with dignity and respect. I feel proud that people know me, seek my help, and acknowledge it. I derive satisfaction from advising my fellow villagers, which makes them happier. I want other women to step out of their homes, earn their respect due to them, and prove the world wrong by showing that they can do anything if they put their minds to it."

The sun had set, and dusk was falling. After talking to Saurabh, I realised what he had meant when, on our bus journey, he had said that it was not about helping women but letting them help themselves. Saurabh, a real change maker, has already set his goals for the future.

He proudly said, "We plan to expand the model to the entire block, form an all-women farmer producers' organization, encourage regenerative agriculture that does not use harmful chemicals, and develop fisheries as an eco-friendly and sustainable livelihood option. I want to see these '*Chasi Bandhus*' as successful entrepreneurs earning money and helping others to earn money sustainably."

It was time for me to return. I had just finished saying goodbye to all, including Saurabh, who had decided to stay back in Lalgarh. I received a call from my wife, "Have you added some money to my Amazon pay account?"

"No", I replied.
"Why didn't you?" she asked.

"I don't know why", I said, "But '*Chasi Bandhus*' are great."

"What was that, who are they?" she snapped.

"I shall explain when I return", I answered and disconnected the call.

Turning the Overturned

(Niraj Kumar & Saheb Bhattacharyya)

For Shadab, this was perhaps the most special incentive for people working at the grassroots level with the community. The community remembers you with respect and fondness, loves you, and misses you after you leave.

The story begins...

On one of the infamous *nawtapa* (a stretch of 9 consecutive hottest days of the year) afternoons of 2012, Vimal, the outgoing team leader of Pradan's Betul project, was briefing his successor, Shadab, on mulberry sericulture. The project anchor, Dinesh, accompanied Shadab. In the tiny office room, on a whiteboard, with flow diagrams, data tables, and many words – haphazardly underlined – Vimal was trying to explain that it was perhaps the right time to close the project. Production was down, the venture was no longer profitable, and participants in the project were withdrawing from it. Dinesh did try to defend the project with a few assertive remarks but conceded in the end. It had been five years since the project to empower the community was initiated in 17 tribal villages. Shadab was in for a shock on the very first day in his office. Although he heard everything Vimal said, he remained silent, suppressing even monosyllabic 'yes' or 'no' as responses.

Madhya Pradesh is not known for mulberry silk production; however, the state government was interested in promoting silk production. *Pradan* joined hands with the state's Directorate of Sericulture to popularise silkworm rearing among the tribal people of the Betul district. In 2008, when the project was started in the village of Padhar, team *Pradan* used its established networks of self-help groups to encourage their members to join the group of farmers engaged in sericulture, growing mulberry to feed silkworms. (Self-help groups are small groups of people with small incomes, all of whom face similar problems, with group members helping one another solve those problems. These groups also regularly encourage their members to set aside small sums of money as savings.) Although most women farmers initially agreed to join, only 43 finally came forward to start a group. Dinesh, hired on contract as a subject-matter specialist since the beginning of the project, was fully convinced of the potential for silkworm production in the area. The villagers found mulberry cultivation to be more profitable because they were assured of the price they would get for the cocoons and the buyer and even of a loan, if required, for any initial investment. Dinesh's conviction, dedication, and hard work saw the group expand steadily: by the end of 2011, the number of farmers associated with silkworm production had gone up to 218.

Three days after taking over as a team leader, Shadab invited Dinesh to discuss the future of the mulberry project and, after they had exchanged greetings, began with two questions: "What

is the whole story behind this project? What is your take on it?"
Dinesh took a long sip of ice-cold *nimbu-paani* (lime juice) and
said, "We have put in a great deal of hard work. We formed an
association of local mulberry farmers, namely SKSKS, short for
Seemant Krishak Shahtut Krimi Palan Sangh, after holding
several meetings of our self- help groups and explaining to the
members the possible benefits of silkworm production. The
farmers received full support, including funds, from the State
government. We also trained our members in the techniques of
sericulture. However, production has been down for the last two
years, and members have started leaving. The SKSKS does not
meet up regularly, and even if a meeting is held, there is little
meaningful discussion. Everyone complains of the decreasing
production and poor returns. Some have even withdrawn
formally from the association." Dinesh looked helpless but
continued, "However, I haven't lost hope: if we work in earnest,
we can bring our members back and make the venture
profitable for them." With these words, Dinesh left.

Shadab kept mulling over the situation. He was in a dilemma. No
development professional likes to close down a community-
oriented project during one's tenure; at the same time, the
project no longer enjoyed the community's trust, and even Vimal,
Shadab's predecessor, had recommended winding up the
project. During his visits to the farms of a few of the members,
their disenchantment with the venture had been apparent,
although the mulberry plants were doing well and looked

healthy. Shadab decided to consult Dinesh yet again before making a decision.

This time, Shadab decided to visit the SKSKS office to meet Dinesh. "You have been with the project since its beginning; what will you do if the decision is left to you?" Shadab asked Dinesh.

The response was instantaneous and firm: "I will try to make the project a success." "What makes you so confident?" asked Shadab.

This time Dinesh took some time before answering. "I have seen mulberry plants, and silkworms grow, also, I have worked with the state-owned silk federation. I have full faith in these women farmers". Dinesh, however, added, "The final decision is always yours." Shadab, an experienced professional, could judge from Dinesh's body language that he was more confident than his words indicated. "Well, then," said Shadab, "You take it forward." After Shadab left, Dinesh stared at the flow chart showing each step in mulberry silkworm production and lapsed into deep thought.

The following day, instead of going to his office, Dinesh called on Kamla *bai*, one of the older but active members of the SKSKS. She was one of the experienced members of the group and had been one of its founder members. They spoke for nearly two hours. After Kamla *bai*, Dinesh decided to see one of the retired agriculture officers with considerable experience in silkworm production and processing. Finally, In the late afternoon,

Dinesh requested a couple of group members to inform all the community leaders that a meeting would be held the next day at 11.30 a.m. at the association's office.

The next day, Dinesh reached his office at 9 in the morning and began by drawing a few circles and arrows on the whiteboard. Shadab joined him soon after, and they began discussing the diagram on the board. By the time the members started coming in, the entire board was covered with sketches and writing.

Seeing thin attendance, Dinesh decided to wait for some more time and invited each one for tea. "The tea is hot, so it would be better if we first have our tea."

Shadab was pleasantly surprised to see Dinesh being on first-name terms with every member and discussing their personal matters comfortably with some. Unfortunately, waiting for some extra time did not yield the result. Only 15 members were in attendance for the meeting.

Undeterred by the poor turnout, Dinesh began: "Sabse pahle *sabhi beheno ko Sitaram*", and then continued, "*mujhe aapko ye batane mein khushi ho rahi hai ki hamne, aap sabo ke taraf se ye faisala kiya hai ki hum SKSKS ko dubara takatwar banyenge aur bina kuch extra kharcha kiye jyada munafa kamayenge. Aur hamne ye faisala, Shadab bhaiya, Kamla bai, or Vaigyanik ji se miljul kar, vichaar vimarsh kar ke liya hai.* (First, greetings to all my sisters! I am happy to inform you that we, on behalf of all of you, have decided to strengthen our group once again and earn more profit without spending any extra amount. And this I have decided in consultation with

Shadab *Bhai*, Kamla *bai*, and Mr Scientist)".

The members began applauding and smiling. Dinesh admitted in the open meeting that Shadab knew that the road ahead would be difficult but was prepared for it.

Jhunki *bai*, one of the most vocal members, asked, "*Aagey karoge kya, ye to batao.* (Tell us what you would do next.)"

Dinesh replied, "*Aap sab thoda intezaar karo our main ek ek kar ke sab bataunga. Bus aapka sahyog rahna chahiye.* (Please be patient, all of you. I will share everything, but I expect that you all keep supporting the group.)"

Kamla *bai* shouted, "*Manjoor hai*" (Agreed), and then everybody joined the chorus of "*Manjoor hai.*"

Shadab seemed a bit puzzled and muttered, "*Ye kya karega* (What will he do?)"

Under the leadership of Dinesh, a team of six technical experts in silkworm production started visiting village after village, requesting full cooperation for the initiative. In most villages, the participation was less than what the team had expected. However, those who had attended the meeting seemed convinced. Bhagirathi *bai*, of Amagohan village, commented, "*Jab tak Dinesh bhaiya hai tab tak bharosa hai.*" (As long as Dinesh *Bhaiya* is with us, we have faith in the project.) The participating villagers agreed to activate the village-based silk growers' groups, locally known as *Mahila Resham Samitis* (MRS). The credibility that *Pradan* had earned, and Dinesh's popularity among the villagers, became the main reasons the villagers started participating actively in the MRS.

As suggested by the team of experts, the villagers brought down the number of cycles of silkworm production from more than ten to four. (Each cycle is one generation of silkworms, from eggs to the cocoons, which are the source of silk: the cocoons are boiled, which means no adult ever emerges from them.) Fewer cycles also saved resources, and the cocoons were of better quality and produced more silk. Once again, the villagers had got going, and the difference in their mood was palpable.

During one of her visits to the SKSKS office, Kamla bai commented, *"Resham ka kaam phir chal para. Aapne to jaadu kar diya gaon walon par.* (We are producing silk once again. You have cast your magic spell on the villagers and have charmed them into working.)"

Dinesh replied, *"Ye hamaarein plan ka pahla part hai.* (This is the first part of my plan.)" Although neither Kamla nor Shadab said a word, their raised eyebrows and smiles said it all.

After successfully convincing the community members and ensuring that mulberry cultivation continued according to the plan, Dinesh focused on the *chawki* rearing centre (CRC, a facility for rearing silkworms; *chawki* are freshly hatched and very young silkworms) and mulberry saplings, the two most crucial inputs for production of quality silk.

The state- owned Silk Federation managed the CRCs, and Dinesh knew that entering the domain of the silk federation would be a challenge and a risk. The Federation was the only silk-procuring agency and offered many incentives to the growers. However, silkworms coming from the government-run CRCs were of poor quality. Often, worms of mixed varieties were supplied to the farmers. Further, negligence in the first few days of the life of silkworms resulted in very high mortality later. Dinesh wanted to set up a few more CRCs so that rearing became decentralised and the entire production system easier to coordinate and manage. Furthermore, he wanted to ensure that production was synchronised across all the silk growers' groups so that it could be easily pooled and sold as one lot.

So far, the plant nursery managed by the Directorate of Sericulture had been supplying mulberry saplings to all the members. However, with time, the quality of samplings went down. The growers had started to complain that saplings provided by the directorate took more than a year to produce enough leaves for feeding silkworms. Dinesh wanted this too to be decentralised. His plan was to set up a nursery in every village, managed by SKSKS members from the respective village.

Dinesh had expected the government to invest in establishing new CRCs and in the village nurseries. He had also expected the government to hand over the management of the CRCs and the nurseries to SKSKS. It was a tall order because it so happened that the same person headed the Directorate of Sericulture (which funded and supported silkworm cultivation in other ways) and the Silk Federation (which was the sole buyer of the final product). This made Shadab suggest to Dinesh that he be extra careful and strategic in his approach. Dinesh thought for some time and said, "Yes, you are right. Still, I have to get the funds and then the management of the CRCs and nurseries. I have to find some way to convince the boss." Dinesh enjoyed an excellent rapport with the General Manager (GM) of Madhya Pradesh Silk Federation (who was also the Assistant Director, Sericulture). Dinesh considered him as somebody with whom one could reason and someone who was also influential. Dinesh wasted no time in calling on the official. After exchanging pleasantries, Dinesh informed the GM about the SKSKS and how the all-women silk farmers' groups had been rejuvenated. The GM thanked Dinesh for his efforts and congratulated him on his success.

Dinesh then politely submitted: "Sir, I have a plan to provide better-quality inputs at cheaper rates, ultimately increasing productivity and income, which will also help the federation get good-quality silk in sufficient quantity and focus on value addition. However, I need full support from the government and officers like you. If you permit, I can share the plan with you."

"Please go ahead", responded the GM.

Dinesh then explained his proposal in detail, spelling out his reasons and mentioning the possible benefits. The GM asked Dinesh to develop a concrete plan and a budget for infrastructure development (the CRCs and the nurseries). Dinesh left the meeting with hope in his heart.

After two weeks, Dinesh and Shadab were requested to call on the Managing Director (MD), Madhya Pradesh Silk Federation, for a meeting. As the earlier meeting had gone well, both Shadab and Dinesh were hopeful of a positive outcome. However, they knew the government bureaucracy well enough not to take anything for granted. Both Dinesh and Shadab reached the MD's office in time and were soon joined by the GM, who greeted them with a smile and requested them to join him in waiting for the MD to call them into his chamber. Dinesh introduced Shadab to the GM, and the conversation turned to the different projects undertaken by *Pradan* in the state of Madhya Pradesh. However, the GM did not mention the specific proposal, and Dinesh grew increasingly restless. Eventually, the MD arrived.

As he ushered the party of three into his office, he looked at his watch and said, "Let us have some tea." The GM introduced Dinesh and Shadab to the MD and briefed him about their efforts to mobilise the community to resume silkworm production with vigour.

The MD, impressed by the account, asked, "How are you so confident that you will be able to handle both CRCs and the nurseries?" Dinesh had his short answer ready: "Sir, I am confident due to two reasons, first, our team at Pradan, and the second and more important, the enthusiasm and the skills of the members of the SKSKS."

Tea was served, and, after taking a sip, the MD said, "We have seen your proposal, we have discussed it among ourselves, and finally, we have decided to accept it as proposed. So, congratulations! Now, make sure that more and more people join and that our district becomes one of the leading clusters of silk production in Madhya Pradesh."

Watching everybody, including the MD, smiling – but not Dinesh, whose face showed a totally different expression – Shadab couldn't stop himself. With everybody still looking on, Shadab stood up and hugged Dinesh. He said, "Sir, Dinesh has given his blood and sweat for this project, and he plans to take it forward. Thank you so much." MD seemed satisfied.

The next day, at 10.30 a.m., more than 30 women members waited eagerly for their Dinesh Bhai. After receiving a call from Dinesh, Kamla bai had called on everyone the previous evening to request their presence. Dinesh broke the news, "Please listen to my plan. Now we will have more than one CRCs, and we will manage all. Also, we will have more than one nursery, and we will manage them all." All the members shouted *"Jai ho"* as Dinesh continued.

"To start the first CRC, we need a small piece of land, and soon, because—" but even before Dinesh could complete the sentence, Kamla *bai* interrupted him and said, "Take my land for the CRC." Dinesh said, "Thank you all for being with me. This development is what I had been waiting for, and now we are halfway to success."

With help from the Directorate of Sericulture, the first CRC came up in Chhuri, on Kamla *bai*'s land. The Centre could incubate 14,000 disease-free layings [eggs] at a time (more than the government-owned CRCs; one laying comprises 500 eggs). The day on which the first CRC was officially opened was a day of celebration for the women members of SKSKS. Dinesh proposed that Kamla be the Centre Manager, and everyone accepted the idea in one voice. Kamla's eyes filled with tears of happiness: she was happy not because she was going to earn more – her wages as the manager – but because her land was being used for the benefit of her fellow villagers. SKSKS soon set up nurseries in three more villages. Dinesh meticulously worked out operational strategies for every front-end and back-end process with a detailed plan in hand. In 2013-14, the community could achieve all that had been planned. Cocoon production increased two fold over that in 2012-13, from 13 tonnes to 26 tonnes; the member producers' average income also increased correspondingly, from Rs 11,000 to Rs 28,000, which was well beyond Dinesh and members had hoped for. Next year, production increased to 45 tonnes, and the income nearly doubled. Kamla *bai* outperformed most others: in 2013-14, she earned nearly Rs 70,000 from cocoon production and another Rs 50,000 from *chawki* rearing.

From an acre of irrigated land, an average farmer earned around Rs 25,000–30000 by growing maize and wheat—it seemed that *acche din waapas aa gaye the* (good days were back again).

Dinesh had been working for eight years but continued to be on contract, and his salary was not commensurate with his experience and hard work. He was looking for opportunities to earn a decent salary. *Pradan* was unable to offer him a competitive salary. One of the reputed developmental organisations offered him a job with substantially higher pay and a workplace closer to his hometown.

Dinesh shared this news with Shadab, who tried to assure Dinesh that he would try to find out something better in a couple of months. Shadab realised that Dinesh deserved a better salary and, as a subject-matter specialist on contract, his opportunities to grow were limited. The villagers were shocked: they never wanted Dinesh to leave SKSKS. Dinesh had become emotionally attached to the project and the people and was keen to see the project becoming sustainable.

Many villagers were at Betul railway station to see Dinesh off. Handing him a bottle of cold drink, Shadab said, *"Jab bhi man kare wapas aa jana.* (Come back whenever you feel like it.)"
Dinesh replied, *"Pakka, guruji.* (Definitely, Sir)".

Shadab then held two rounds of discussion with all the SKSKS and MRS active members about the project. He noted that the members were missing Dinesh, and the activities had begun to suffer for want of a personal touch.

About three and half months later, Shadab was bidding farewell to another colleague at a party. Shadab's mobile rang. He went outside for a better signal. It was Dinesh, and Shadab was happy to hear Dinesh's voice. "So, how are you?", asked Shadab. *"Theek hun guruji lekin ab wapas aana padega."* (I am fine, Sir, but I will have to return.) *"Bai log baar baar call kar rahe hai aur wapas aane ke liye bol rahe hai* (The womenfolk keep calling me, insisting that I return.) *"To aa ja"* (Come back, then) was Shadab's instant response.

For Shadab, this aspect was perhaps the most special incentive for people working at the grassroots level with community. The community remembers you with respect and fondness, loves you, and misses you after you leave. And if Dinesh comes back, it would be because of the community, and because of Dinesh's sense of responsibility as a development professional

towards the community. Shadab initiated the formal process for making an offer and providing for Dinesh's salary in the budget. Dinesh was already at the SKSKS office a few days before Shadab had thought of and was refering the papers he had prepared for the revival of silkworm production without waiting for any official confirmation from *Pradan*. Dinesh's second inning was more intense and vigorous. In consultation with Shadab, he decided to set up a separate business enterprise around mulberry silkworm rearing. The enterprise's planned core business was cocoon production, aggregation, and sale to Madhya Pradesh Silk Federation.

Dinesh once again started reaching out to the MRS and requested them to take the lead in identifying and shortlisting new farmers interested in sericulture. Women groups on their own prepared a detailed checklist to assess new applicants by adding one new question: whether the applicant would be ready to take up silkworm rearing even before any assistance from the government was available? Notably, the groups succeeded in putting this policy into practice. By the end of 2014-

15, out of 600 farmers seeking membership, 377 were finally inducted by different MRS. In consultation with the growers' representatives, a production system was finalized, making it more competitive and predictable.

By 2015-16, the membership of SKSKS had increased to 724, and production had gone up to 145 tonnes. The group began to believe that it needed a more formal institution, a business plan, and a management information system to keep track of the details of all the activities and financial transactions.

After several rounds of consultation with the member farmers, experts, and the State government's Commissioner for Sericulture, a farmer-producer company was considered the most appropriate option. Thus, on 15 September 2016, the first all-woman farmer-producer company of Madhya Pradesh, namely the Satpuda Women Silk Producer Company Ltd (SWSPCL) came into existence, with Dinesh as the CEO of the enterprise, following his resignation from *Pradan*.

Even before Dinesh could celebrate establishing a member-owned company and the owners could sell their first harvest, they received a blow: the Silk Federation field staff went on an indefinite strike. In 5 days, 30 tonnes of raw cocoons, worth Rs 75 lakh was expected from 700 farmers—and its only buyer in the market was on strike. For Dinesh, the company's CEO, nothing could have been more catastrophic. He was helpless as substantial financial resources were at stake. It seemed impossible to find an alternative market within even 15 days.

Dinesh and Shadab approached the CEO of Betul Zilla Panchayat (the Betul District Council), seeking his intervention to ensure that the Silk Federation honoured its commitment to buy the cocoons. An hour later, Shadab called the Commissioner of Sericulture, and briefed him on the situation. The Commissioner listened patiently and assured Shadab that the procurement would happen as planned.

Although the Federation finally bought all the cocoons, Dinesh realized that such total reliance on a single source might not be the best option for SWSPCL to grow. SWSPCL started contacting potential buyers from Tamil Nadu, Karnataka, and West Bengal, even as the Federation struggled with internal conflicts.

Afterword

In November 2017, SWSPCL managed to sell 30 tonnes of cocoons (out of 56 tonnes) to a trader in Bangalore at a price that was 12% higher than that offered by the Silk Federation. On learning of this deal, the new Commissioner of Sericulture was furious and shot off a letter to *Pradan*'s head office, raising concerns over financial misappropriation by the local *Pradan* team. *Pradan* responded with details of benefits the farmers had earned by selling cocoons in the open market. Dinesh remained firm on his decision and continued to build new market links. Many of the old buyers of the federation turned to

SWSPCL for raw materials. These buyers realised that dealing with SWSPCL was more transparent and hassle-free. The successful journey continued, and SWSPCL kept crossing one milestone after another. The temporary impasse turned out to be a blessing in disguise.

Dinesh was happier, Shadab was celebrating, and *Pradan* was proud—not because Dinesh had realised his dream but because more than 700 tribal women had become successful entrepreneurs running their own enterprises. Kamla *bai* was now a role model for many women across the districts, and SWSPCL had the distinction of being one of the most successful women farmer-producer companies in India. The State government and *Pradan*, encouraged by the success, planned to replicate a similar experiment in nearby districts as well. Already there's talk of setting up egg production centres.

*****

Aksham se Saksham

(Satyendra Nath Mishra & Shibam Jha)

"Jaha kabhi kuch nahi hota tha, jaha log bahar jaa ke majdoori kia karte thee, aaj ke din hum logo ko bahar see bula ke sammaan see kaam dete hain. Ye jeevan ka sabse bada badlaav hai."

Sanjay Markam, 24,
A villager from Guhannala

The story begins...

Shivam, a young professional at Pradan, woke up early, his face awash in the morning sunlight, in the mud house in Guhannala village that had been his home for the last five-odd years, during which he had seen the village being transformed. Sparkling dewdrops on the lush green leaves of trees and bamboo shoots growing around the house made him smile— which vanished the next moment by the sudden realisation that today was his last working day in the village. Tears rolled down his cheeks, but whether of happiness or pain, he could not say.

Guhannala, a small village of no more than 200 households, lies along a state highway in the Dhamtari district of Chhattisgarh. Guhannala was set up in 1952 to resettle those displaced from the Mahanadi catchment area following the construction of the Dudhawa dam nearby. The villagers used to boast that Guhannala was the head of the king cobra on which rested the dam, a smaller version of the mythical *Sheshnaag* that supports the Earth according to Hindu mythology.

However, settling on this previously forested land had not been easy. It was an undulating, rocky, and barren expanse that confronted the displaced as they arrived. And the water was scarce, as though Mother Nature was mocking and challenging them. The 85-year-old Samari *Dadi* recalled, *"Humaan din bhaar ke butaa bhar jab at rahenn, tab hamaar paas sirf madia pench (a liquid bowl of rice and dry vegetable) ke saadhan rahise. Din bhar maati la samtali karen aur apan rahe bhar Guhannala la banayein* (We used to have only a bowl of 'media pench' (a local rice flour dish) to sustain us as we struggled to make Guhannala habitable)."

It took hard labour of more than a quarter of a century to level the land to make it fit for farming. However, to depend on the erratic and unpredictable rainfall for agriculture was a gamble. Although the village lay between two streams, one to the north and one to the south, the village remained dry most of the year because it had no way of storing water.

Life was tough from the beginning and became more challenging every year. Adults began migrating to other villages or cities to earn a living, and pawning what little jewellery they had was among the limited options open to them if they were to survive. Heera Bhai, a long- time resident, put it succinctly when he said that migration was their fate, and Guhannala would soon be barren once again.

The situation continued to worsen after the 1990s. Given the lack of irrigation, one crop of rice a year, with its low and erratic yields, was the sole source of sustenance for the village. Most households had a piece of farmland as their backyard but could grow nothing. Many young men from the village had migrated to other states, mainly Maharashtra, Gujarat, and Andhra Pradesh. The prolonged absence of menfolk made life even more difficult for the women, who were left to take care of the elderly and the children in addition to the usual household chores.

Samari *bai* said: *"mahila mann la ye samay bahut pareshani la jhelna padish. Humaan ha koshish karat rahen ki kam paisa me kaise chala sakein mahino mahino ke baad ye mann kama ke aye to ghar ke samaan le paat rahein* (For women, those days were tough. We tried hard to run the house with the meagre money we had. After many months when men, who migrated for work, returned to the village, we were able to purchase anything)."

As Shivam, who worked with Pradan, pondered over the situation, he recalled what Dhananjay Pandey, the official from NABARD, the National Bank for Agriculture and Rural Development, had once said. Pandey's assessment was that the villagers lacked proper organisational support to manage their resources, make farming more productive, and generate other options for earning a living. Shivam, too, believed that the village had potential which had never been utilised.

Shivam appealed to Pandey for help. "Sir, I see ample scope for development, but I don't know what to do; I need a concrete plan and a road map of its implementation", said Shivam.

One Saturday, Dhananjay Pandey and Shivam visited the village to meet the sarpanch (the village chief) and village panchayat members (the village committee) to explore possible interventions. The barren backyard farms immediately caught their attention. "Why are the backyard farms barren?" asked Dhananjay. Samita, a woman in her 30s, responded, "What can we do? We do not have saplings; we do not have water, and we do not know what can come up well under these conditions." After the meeting, Dhananjay requested Shivam for more details about the village.

Shivam did not have to wait for long for his phone to ring: "Hello Shivam, this is Dhananjay. I have discussed the matter with my boss and have shared all the details you sent. We will be happy to help the people of Guhannala under our 'waadi' scheme (a scheme to promote kitchen gardens or backyard farms, waadi being the local term for such parcels of land)." Shivam was more than happy. "Thank you, Sir", he responded and promised to meet the bank official soon to understand more about the scheme. "Looking forward to that; you may have to work harder now", replied Dhananjay.

Although the village women were hard-working, they had little experience working as a group or as a collective. They agreed to form 'sakhi mandals (all-women friend circles or self-help groups) but remained unaware of their functioning and objectives.

Draupadi didi said, *"Haman la bhaiya mann jod ke chal ge aur khata khulwa daalein lekin khana khula ke Karna Kaise hai wo samjh nahi aata"* (Maybe, with some help, we opened a bank account, but what next? We do not know how to operate a bank account).

Shivam's new tasks were now making greater demands on him. He was convinced that the women wanted to bring about a change and lead but needed somebody to guide them.

In her 50s and a particularly active executive member of the newly formed *sakhi mandal*, Samari didi was candid enough to admit its shortcomings: "We have everything, but our *sakhis* [women members] cannot gather the courage to come together to do something."

Despite his experience in Pradan, Shivam found it challenging to overcome the reluctance of the women members and to instil in them a feeling of solidarity, of belonging. He realised that it was difficult for women to trust outsiders; they were weary and found it hard to believe that a stranger wanted to organise them not for his benefit but to further their well-being. Shivam understood that the reasons behind the women's hesitation to come forward, take on a leadership role, and be willing to extend the horizons of their existence were deep-rooted: something more drastic was called for to bring about the change.

In 2015, Guhannala had 15 self-help groups and one village organisation representing 179 households, but these existed only on paper. For Shivam, it was a test of his professionalism. These groups needed to become functional. A great deal was expected of him, and he was scared.

With the support of his team members, 'didi's (executive members of the *sakhi mandals*), and a few villagers, Shivam ensured that each household in Guhannala, especially the most vulnerable ones, was part of a self-help group. In a very short span of time, he noticed some change among the members. The meetings became more regular, and Shivam was delighted to see how keen a few members were to learn and assume leadership. Members of the groups were enthusiastic about participating in the *waadi* scheme, through which they were given saplings of fruit trees, including mango and cashew. Shivam ensured that the executive members and his colleagues from Pradan regularly visited all the members and remained in touch with them. The newly planted trees and other seasonal crops in the backyard farms made the villagers happy, and they started valuing the *sakhi mandals* more. Shashikant, a colleague of Shivam, said to him, "Shivam, you have set the ball rolling; now we must ensure that momentum is maintained."

The *waadi* project seemed to work but had not been particularly effective in improving the economic well-being of the people. The residents of Guhannala remained poor. The average landholding in Guhannala was about 1.5 hectares, but most of it was barren because there was no water to irrigate the land. The villagers now wanted to know what they could grow, how to farm more efficiently using modern methods, and who was to make the initial investment. After a detailed discussion, organic farming was considered the most feasible option.

Shivam soon realised that although he wanted to promote organic farming, a far more severe problem for the villagers was getting enough water for the household, let alone irrigating the fields. "How will agriculture be sustainable in this situation?" Shivam kept asking himself as he thought of Guhannala. It appeared to him that he was peeling an onion: as the team tackled one problem, another one came to the fore. He said to himself, "Maybe this is one of the reasons why bringing in a socio-economic change in any community is so difficult."

In March 2017, when a meeting of villagers was called to discuss ways of overcoming water scarcity, the villagers appeared overwhelmed: they had never been consulted before on such matters. Each member was given the opportunity to offer suggestions. But, it was Draupadi Markam, whose voice became the majority's voice. She highlighted the importance of 'ekeekrit prakirtik sansadhan ka upyog' (integrated management of natural resources) for Guhannala. She called upon all the members to work together for such integration. The members agreed that with collective efforts, they can manage their natural resources, especially water, more effectively and that the women of the village stand to benefit the most from such actions.

For Shivam, actual work on the ground was just starting. He discussed with his colleague the possible approaches and frameworks that would work in Guhannala. His colleagues suggested that Shivam should look at Chhindbharri, a village in the same district. Pradan had turned that into a model village, demonstrating how natural resources could be managed sustainably. Shivam knew that replicating a model that had worked for one village blindly in another could be disastrous. To ensure community participation, people must understand what they need to do and why. Sunita *didi*, a respected member of one of the self-help groups, was made responsible for selecting a team of 15 from the village to visit Chhindbharri. The team was joined by representatives of Pradan, block and district-level officials, and the secretary of the gram panchayat, and all visited Chhindbharri together.

Although it is common for group members to share their experiences once they return from any educational tour, the tone and the content of the discussion that followed the visit surprised Shivam. The tone was collaborative, and the content was both new and re-energised.

One of the officials remarked, "I have never met such an enthusiastic group. Everybody was ready to take responsibility and help others. It seems these women are veterans, and they know their job well." The visit made everyone realise that they needed to work together if Guhannala had to transform into a model village.

"It is not going to be an easy time ahead, " said Shivam, smiling.

Land development and building storage structures for water were the first activities according to the new plan developed by team Guhannala. And both were completed far ahead of schedule. State departments dealing with horticulture, agriculture, and animal husbandry came forward and offered to introduce various developmental schemes of their respective departments in the village. Shivam and his team had to ensure that no work was duplicated and that all the resources were used optimally. The central government's employment guarantee scheme, MGNREGA, saw the best utilisation of funds for village development. The local Pradan camp office had become the most happening place in the village. The idea to pool the funds, technical expertise and local wisdom to convert the barren lands into fertile fields with rich potential had proven successful.

The changing relations between all the actors were succinctly captured by Chandra Prakash Sahu of the horticulture department, "The kind of engagement Pradan is showing in the village is commendable. One difference from our approach is the kind of relationship these young professionals make. Our actions were also changed because of the villagers' interaction with the organisation and us. They have managed to generate trust among the community members."

Although all seemed to be going well, a conflict soon surfaced over the development of a patch of land to demonstrate how integrated natural resource management works. Every member wanted the demonstration plot to be on their land. The village split into smaller groups, each demanding priority for their patch of land.

Shivam decided not to intervene and left the decision to the villagers and members of the *sakhi mandals*. After a few rounds of talks, a consensus emerged that work should begin on the area that lay at a higher elevation.

"Understanding the process of turning a piece of barren land into a cultivable patch brought all the members on the same page, and they agreed to initiate the work from the upper end of the tract", explained the local agriculture officer.

Although it took time, the decision was democratic, and the villagers believed in completing the work collectively. In the process, Shivam could trace the essence of a collective effort among the villagers.

In 2018, a new window of opportunity presented itself. Some funds were available at the district level to develop orchards on barren lands. Earlier, a similar plan was not implemented for want of funds. Shivam noted that villagers were now more proactive and more open and willing to engage with other actors, adopt, and try, one step at a time-all of it as a collective. People were comfortable talking to government officials and professionals and could easily communicate what they needed.

Afterword

By the early 2020s, villagers converted roughly 40 hectares of the additional area into arable land, of which 28 hectares were under various crops like rice, oilseeds, lemon, papaya, karonda, and drumstick. About 45 water-harvesting structures were built and managed by the village to ensure that water from run-off served to recharge groundwater. Access to a pond provided fishery as a complementary source of livelihood. With government funding and professional support, villagers started exploring techniques like drip irrigation, sprinkler irrigation, and trellises for cultivating vegetables. Support from the H T Parekh Foundation served as a catalyst. The villagers converted about 5 hectares of additional not-so-fertile land into a patch of community land to grow vegetables. People of Guhannala no longer migrated in search of work, and skilled artisans started getting offers of higher wages. Shivam was happy to read the findings of a study carried out by an independent agency that the average annual household income in Guhannala had increased from Rs. 47,172 to Rs. 89,652 between 2015 and 2021.

Young girls who had left the village as brides were pleasantly surprised when they visited the village after a couple of years. The landscape had been transformed, and prosperity was noticeable. Access to water, sanitation, food, fodder, and fuelwood and higher wages for young adults had changed the face of the village.

Shivam learnt that Pradan was planning to transfer him to another village, which he would begin to transform as he did to Guhannala. The impending move prompted him to recapitulate his experiences and list his learnings. The list ran thus - Merely forming self- help groups does not automatically result in their members working together; leadership can be encouraged, nurtured, and promoted; even a single idea or individual can trigger change, as Draupadi Markam proved in Guhannala; and seeing the success of others with the same background gives confidence to the rest that they too can succeed; and lastly Creating a community infrastructure facilitates, reinforces, and motivates a community to work as a team or as a village organisation. However, what gave Shivam maximum satisfaction – something that he would cherish forever – was the love and trust of the villagers, colleagues, and government officials. The words of Draupadi Markam sum up the story of a changed Guhannala, particularly the women of Guhannala.

"Human la vishwas nahi rahise ki ate bade adhikari mann ke saamne Haman kucho bol paabo ki nahi, lekin jab koi kaam me ache se judge to koi ke saamne bole me dar ni laage, ye samjh ban paayis. (We never thought that we one day we'd be able to speak to a senior official: your good work gives you confidence—and that has been our major learning)."

The newly built office of the village organisation, a source of income for women's self-help groups, is now the hub of non-farm activities. The district administration is proud of this community-owned asset, the most preferred venue for training. Trainees get the opportunity to meet and learn from the experiences of local heroes who have changed the traditional definition of community leadership. Many members of the self-help groups are now engaged in making candles, soaps, and detergents and plan to sell them in local markets. Women in Guhannala are now an economic pillar of their family and the village. Women members have a few business plans of their own. Although Shivam will be no longer around to encourage the village's women leaders, the spirit of thinking, planning, and working collectively is here to stay. The way Shivam nurtured leadership in the women has taught him how to empower women elsewhere.

Shivam didn't realise that his tears had dried, and a smile had lit up his face. He thought it was time to have his breakfast before packing up and leaving Guhannala, perhaps never to return.

*****

Strive Struggle and Success

(Indirah Indibara & Jyoti Rekha Roy Pradhan)

As soon as the MLA finished his speech, Niru, with all her courage, went up the stage, looked at the MLA and exhorted, "Women need not bow down their heads. Rather, they need to hold their heads high and walk."

The story begins...

April 2004: Namita, an agile and cheerful lady, had been silent for some days. His neighbours and fellow members of the self-help group (SHG) in Karanjia block of Mayurbhanj district of Odisha were surprised to see the change in the behaviour of one of the most active members. Seeing her alone and sitting quietly under a mango tree, Seema and Swarna, two of the members of her group, approached her and asked, *"what is the reason you seem very sad"*?

Namita tried to put on a brave face and said, *"nothing, just wanted to be alone"*.

Not satisfied with the answer, Swarna went down to her knees, lifted her face, looked in her eyes said, *"Namita, you are hiding something from us. Please let us know; we shall try to help you out."*

Listening to these sentences from one of her close friends, she broke down into tears and started crying.

Namita used to live with her in-laws. They were a joint family. Her husband is the younger of the two brothers. One day when all the family members were out of home, her brother-in-law took undue advantage of her. She complained to her husband and mother-in-law. The husband was furious and fought with his brother. However, unfortunately, her mother- in-law and sister-in-law sternly warned her not to discuss this matter with anyone.

"I feel suffocated in the house, and I fear for my life as the culprit is still in the house and has not changed. I have lost my self-esteem and cannot face anyone." said Namita, sobbing. This left Seema and Swarna red-faced, more with shame and less anger.

The news spread in the village like a wildfire, and the village was divided into two groups. One group comprising of a few SHG leaders wanted justice for Namita and wanted her to fight. In contrast, most of the villagers, including men, and women, young and old, raised a question about her character and suggested that she should do everything to save her family from disgrace. Namita, already in shock, was further torn between the devil and the deep blue sea. The issue was discussed at various levels of the SHG collectives. Unfortunately, discussions did not result in any action. Instead, many questions started bothering most members – Are they all spineless? Will they ever stand up for themselves or their sisters? Does their organisation have the capacity to better their lives?

Professional Assistance for Development Action (Pradan), set up in 1983, started its operation in the Karanjia block of Mayurbhanj district in 2000. The primary focus was mobilising tribal and other marginalised women and forming small saving and credit groups known as self-help groups (SHGs). SHGs would help the women to enhance their income through adopting improved practices in agriculture and other livelihood activities. Though cases similar to Namita's were also being reported earlier, none had formally informed their groups. But after Namita reported the issue and the villagers couldn't do much, Jyoti, the project head in Mayurbhanj, started reflecting on her organisation's role.

"We can't sit idle and watch women members being harassed, discriminated and beaten. So, we discussed the same with the clusters' representatives and realised the need for a separate institution at the block level", informed Jyoti.

Before Namita's story came to the fore, 25 village-level clusters were formed. The representatives of each cluster came together at the block level to discuss the issue of women security and empowerment and decided to form a block-level federation. The organisation was named "Sampurnna", – meaning complete and self-reliant.

"We didn't have our own office space, and we started our office in a small corner of the Pradan office with only one table and chair", said Jyoti.

Since its formation, Sampurnna has grown as an organisation and has worked to promote livelihood among the poor helpless women, entitlement in government schemes, participation of women in local governance, and against domestic violence.

"To protect women's rights, we had to fight with our male counterparts, block-level officers and some time with our own women members", informed Niru, one of the active members of the federation.

In the Mahadhivesan (an annual gathering of all women members of Sampurnna) held in 2009-10, various block and district level officials were invited. The local member of the legislative assembly (MLA) was the chief guest on occasion. When the MLA started suggesting that women follow the traditional culture and respect social norms during his inaugural address, resentment was evident among the participating members. However, members kept their anger in control. However, as soon as he commented that 'good women were supposed to be in purdah with their heads bowed', members who had come together to celebrate their lives and success stories were furious. The address, no doubt, did not go down well.

As soon as the MLA finished his speech, Niru, with all her courage, went up the stage, looked at the MLA and exhorted, "Women need not bow down their heads. Rather, they need to hold their heads high and walk". Thunderous applause welcomed his strong retort to the MLA.

"We feel proud when we say that we have not bowed down since then", informed Jyoti.

Sampurna was getting stronger, and the cause it espoused was gaining traction among the community, particularly among the women members. Jyoti had formed an informal committee to educate women regarding their rights and duties.

Like any other woman in the village of Jhalkiani in the Mayurbhanj district, Malati had to work hard to sustain herself and her family. She worked as an agricultural labourer and later learnt tile roofing to increase her income. On the other hand, her husband, a drunkard, spent his time on his farm doing nothing or sleeping at home. The total income of the family was insufficient to meet the household expenses. Whenever Malti objected to his drinking, he would shout and threaten to beat her.

Malti joined Sampurnna and started taking a keen interest in the federation's activities. Seeing her interest in community work, Jyoti encouraged Malti to file nominations for the position of ward member1 during the panchayat election. Malati filed her nomination for the post of ward member. Despite strong resistance from her brother-in-law, she fought for election, and she was elected. Encouraged by her victory, she started giving more time to social work in the village. She played a crucial role in initiating integrated natural resource management (INRM), a govern run scheme. Jyoti once again requested her to take the role of the INRM cluster leader of the Karanjiya block.

As a mate under the MGNREGA, Malti led the women volunteers to create awareness about citizens' rights and grievances. Within a couple of months, 50 complaints were filed by the villagers against irregularities in MGNREGA payment. Buoyed by her success,

Malti supported and encouraged other women to work for Panchayat and groomed five more women as MGNREGA mates.

Despite her professional success, Malti's husband continued to abuse her mentally, and she sought the support of Sampurnna to handle the situation. Jyoti and a few other members visited her house and met her husband first separately and then with Malti.

Despite her professional success, Malti's husband continued to abuse her mentally, and she sought the support of Sampurnna to handle the situation. Jyoti and a few other members visited her house and met her husband first separately and then with Malti.

Listening to her husband, even otherwise strong Malti broke down.

"If you don't change, Sampurnna will go to the police and complain against you", threatened Jyoti.

Though Malti's husband did not change entirely but stopped beating and threatening her. Malti actively discussed domestic violence issues in the village and encouraged women not to bend.

She continued to do the roof tiling work. She availed a loan under the housing scheme and built a house of her own.

Sampurnna was celebratory after what they called 'one more woman (Malti) freed from the sufferings'. Though SHGs were doing well in making financially literate and independent, they

---

[1] Every village Panchayat is divided into wards, i.e. smaller areas. Each ward elects a representative known as the Ward Member (Panch), who gets a fixed salary from the government.

upped the ante to end gender-based discrimination and violence in the areas of their influence. Members moved from one hamlet to another to raise awareness against gender discrimination.

"If you don't change, Sampurnna will go to the police and complain against you", threatened Jyoti.

Though Malti's husband did not change entirely but stopped beating and threatening her. Malti actively discussed domestic violence issues in the village and encouraged women not to bend. She continued to do the roof tiling work. She availed a loan under the housing scheme and built a house of her own.

Sampurnna was celebratory after what they called 'one more woman (Malti) freed from the sufferings'. Though SHGs were doing well in making financially literate and independent, they upped the ante to end gender-based discrimination and violence in the areas of their influence. Members moved from one hamlet to another to raise awareness against gender discrimination.

During one of the regular meetings of the federation, Malti suggested, "Now we should provide full support to all the women facing violence and continue to support them till they get justice".

Jyoti liked the idea and decided to take the federation's activities to the next level. In the next 90 days federation established a Women Support Centre (WSC) to provide end to end support to women facing violence. The centre provided counselling support to the distressed women and, if needed, it provided legal support as well.

Malti claimed, "Till today, 15 cases have come to the WSC for counselling and legal support, and I am happy to inform you that all have been resolved" Malti happily narrated her success story. "For me, the story of Latika has been very inspiring; it gives me the satisfaction of doing something fruitful for our sisters and the society", was her concluding sentence.

Latika of Rasamtala village fell in love with Ramesh at the very early age of 16. Although Latika did not inform her parents, they warned her when they came to know about her relationship. She did not budge and married him despite her parent's disapproval. She was not even out of her teen when she became the mother of two sons. She had to quit her studies to take care of her children and family. Unfortunately, after marriage, she realised that her husband considered her an object of sex. Sexual violence became a routine. She kept quiet as she thought that her parents and others would blame her for the suffering. Her husband started beating her with passing days if she resisted his sexual demands. Her resistance to any-time sex was construed as the outcome of her extramarital relations.

Her in-laws, too, did not come to her rescue. Instead, one day they joined Ramesh when he tried to kill her by pouring kerosene. She shouted for help. Fortunately, neighbours responded to her shout and saved her. She wanted to register a police case against her in-laws and husband, but under the pressure of her parents and local villagers, she had to let it go. However, soon the incident became public. Soon she was approached by the members of WSC.

Members advised her to become a member of the SHG and attend various gender awareness camps. She could understand that she needed to speak up against her exploitation. She decided to exert and fight for her rights. She could muster the courage to say NO to anytime sex demands of her husband. She didn't hesitate to join her WSC members to warn her in-laws against any violence against her.

She again resumed her studies. As she still loved her husband, she continued living with her and counselling him to change his behaviour. Very soon, to everyone's surprise, her husband's behaviour changed.

"She is now a role model for all the young girls. Every woman tries to hide her sufferings, but she shared her stories during a mahadhiveshan (general body meeting with invited members) in front of 5000 women. After that, though, she had to face the anger of her in-laws and relatives because she shared her family story in public", informed Jyoti. Latika had become a prominent member of Sampurnna and was one of the most sought-after para-legal counsellors.

Afterword

"Now, women from far-flung villages approach us. Even police and government officers recommend us to distressed women. We know and appreciate the problems faced by our sisters better, and so we are effective and successful," informed Latika.

Federation took the initiative of conducting discussion sessions on gender named "Prajapati" for the students of classes 8 and 9 to make young minds aware of existing gender discrimination and gender-based violence in society. "Because of Covid, the initiative was stopped midway. However, the initial outcomes were very encouraging, and we plan to resume it as early as possible," said Jyoti.

"I feel proud when I share a story about Deep Joshi Sir. He is the visionary founder of Pradanand, a Magsaysay awardee and has inspired many. But during one of our meetings in the Khadikudar village, he asked participating women. "All the benefits of Sampurnna you have articulated says about better SHGs, empowered women, better savings and loan facilities. If we somehow bring the bank near your village, will you still need Sampurnna? I think we may not need Sampurna then." One lady smilingly answered, **"Yes, the bank can do all these things, but can the bank unite these 4000 women, give us our rights, and make us free from all the social discrimination?"** After that, all, including Joshi Sir, had slipped into silence".

This small story, narrated with all the emotions by Jyoti, told everything about the strive, struggle and success of the Sampurna.

*****

The Rebirth of a Professional
(Kumar Thangavelsamy & Shailendra Kumar Singh)

Kamakhya Singh was both shocked and angry. The mukhiya, the head of the village council, had turned down the request of a poor woman for money to repair her house.

The story begins...

Kamakhya Singh had reached his office half an hour early and was busy working on a file that had been lying on his table since the previous day. His phone rang couple of times, but he decided to ignore the call: working on the file was urgent. After a few minutes, when the phone rang again, Kamakhya picked up the receiver and greeted the caller with a rather brusque hello. The call was from his hometown, and he heard a woman sobbing as she explained her situation. Kamakhya Singh was both shocked and angry. The *mukhiya*, the head of the village council, had turned down the request of a poor woman from a disadvantaged community – she belonged to one of the Scheduled Castes – for money to repair her house. The house was severely damaged in the torrential rains the village recently experienced. It was alleged that the mukhiya entertained such requests only from the socially influential or in exchange for a consideration. Kamakhya Singh felt uneasy and drank a full glass of water before returning to the file he had intended to dispose off before lunch.

Kamakhya Singh, a professional with a master's degree in rural development and more than a decade of experience in the social sector, was perturbed with the news he had been getting about the working of the *gram panchayat,* the village council of Pindarkone, the village from which he hailed, in Padma block of Hazaribagh district, Jharkhand. By the following weekend, he was in the village. As he took a walk around it, he found plants growing from the cracks in the wall of the Panchayat Bhawan (the council building). A closer look revealed broken floors and the surroundings full of animal dung. He was dismayed by the overall air of neglect that pervaded the premises. When he discussed the sad situation with the villagers, he was told that the earlier mukhiya had to give up his position because a charge of murder was pending against him. The second-in-command, the deputy mukhiya and the council's secretary managed the show and were corrupt. Kamakhya Singh then spoke his mind: "We need to change this. If necessary, I will stand for the panchayat election."

The villagers were unanimous in their support and requested that he contest the election scheduled for next year. "We want somebody who is committed and educated, and has a clean image, to lead us", said Mewat, who belonged to one of the scheduled castes.

Back in his office, Kamakhya Singh kept mulling over his decision to return to his village and fight the election for a seat on the village council. But that also meant giving up his secured job and entering an unknown territory. The question that kept echoing in his mind was this: *"Kya hum kamyab hongey?"* (Will I be successful?)

Kamakhya Singh bade goodbye to his decade-old job. While others led convoys of their respective supporters in the fleets of 10–15 vehicles during their nomination and spent more than Rs 10 lakh (one million) on campaigning, Kamakhya went on his motorcycle with four of his fellow villagers to file his nomination and his total expenses for electioneering were about Rs 35,000. Young villagers campaigned for Kamakhya Singh voluntarily, with no expectations of any kind, and his experience in the development sector did prove handy in winning the support of his constituency. To his surprise and delight, he won the election. And now, the responsibility for developing the village council and the village itself was on him.

In the absence of a proper building for the *panchayat* (village council), the oath-taking ceremony for the newly elected members was organised in the courtyard of a school. After the ceremony, Kamakhya Singh, the newly elected head of the village council, held a small meeting with the newly elected representatives; in the case of women representatives, their husbands were also invited to attend.

Kamakhya Singh said, "I congratulate each of you. As we have limited resources, we need to prioritise our work and pay more attention to developing the poorer villages such as Bhandara, Bardeva, and Nachanve."

As soon as the newly elected mukhiya, Kamakhya, had concluded his welcome speech, a ward member got up and voiced his reservations: *"Mukhiya Ji,* please allocate the money meant for development equally to all the seven villages within the jurisdiction of this council. It will be unfair to favour only some villages."

Soon, the same sentiment echoed from all directions. Kamakhya Singh tried to convince the members; he said, "We all have been elected to serve all the people equitably, and we should take greater care of those who are poorer and lag." Soon, the meeting became a free for all and had to be ended abruptly.

Within a fortnight of his election, some influential contractors, a few ward members, and other local self-acclaimed political leaders organised a protest rally against Kamakhya Singh. They even instigated the ward members to write to the local block development officer (BDO), Mr Malay Kumar, demanding that Kamakhya Singh be removed. However, the mukhiya remained steadfast in his decision, although he realised that to bring about a substantial change, he needed the support of all the ward members.

The block development officer called a meeting on the school premises. The meeting started at 9 a.m. and continued till 5 p.m.

The development officer repeatedly referred to the Panchayati Raj Act and said: "You cannot remove an elected representative because the public has directly elected him."

Having failed to convince the BDO, the ward members began accusing him of dictatorship and abusing Kamakhya Singh. However, the BDO was firm: "Whether you like him or not, you will have to work with him."

The ward members soon realised that it was better to go by the book. Just before the meeting was to end, a ward member asked, "Will we have our future meetings at this venue, which is unsuitable for the purpose?" Kamakhya Singh seized the opportunity and announced that a better building for the office would be built. Ashok Rana, a council member, extended his support for this project.

Kamakhya Singh then contacted the BDO and the district development commissioner and learnt that the government had already cleared the proposal to construct the Panchayat Bhawan (the building for the council office)—and the building had already been completed (on paper only). Shocked, Kamakhya Singh decided to follow up with the relevant officials with the required facts and photographs. After several rounds of correspondence and personal follow-up by the mukhiya, the fresh proposal, estimated at Rs 15 lakh (about 1.5 million rupees), was approved. Within a year, the building was ready. New furniture including chairs, tables, and a cupboard was also bought. This was a moment of great joy and satisfaction to Kamakhya Singh. The building became a happening place, and Kamakhya started planning for a few more changes.

His success also won him some enemies, who were jealous of his increasing popularity and realised that they were losing their sources of income and influence. A few of the ward members resumed their activities to undermine Singh. This time, they influenced some of the employees of the block office and made the mukhiya's job more difficult. Singh found himself unable to move forward. He met the BDO, who retained his earlier policy: He said,"I will not interfere in the working of democratically elected people's representatives; you have to manage on your own."

With time, work in the panchayat came to a halt. Dismayed, the mukhiya gave up. The newly built council building once again wore a deserted look. Kamakhya Singh, once a committed and dedicated enthusiast, who had left a secure job to develop his village, turned apathetic and withdrew into himself. What a pity that this once-hopeful man had lost all his hopes.

It was a scorching hot afternoon in May. Singh was having his siesta. "Kamakhya Sir, where are you?" shouted somebody from outside.

He came out to find two young men with towels around their heads to keep out the sun. "Sir, we are Shiva and Zanid from Pradan and would like to talk to you", said one of the two, wiping sweat from his face.

The mukhiya was pleased to see them because he had worked with Pradan for more than a decade. He invited them in and offered them cold water from a pitcher. "Please call me Kamakhya and not 'sir'", said Singh and offered them chairs to sit.

"We are working on a capacity-building project for members of village councils (panchayats), and we seek your help in running the project for your panchayat. We have heard a lot about your leadership and panchayat and hence decided to start from Pindarkone–your village–in this block", said Shiva. Sensing Kamakhya's interest, Zanid explained the process in detail. Kamakhya was both impressed and excited. The meeting continued for more than two hours, and the visiting duo seemed satisfied with the outcome.

Next Sunday, all the elected representatives gathered in the Panchayat Bhawan. The dust on the chairs reflected the apathy of the members and the current state of affairs. Although Kamakhya was excited, the members did not appear as hopeful. "Will the situation in our panchayat ever change?" asked one of the members.

Shiva from Pradan explained the modalities of the project and requested the council to sign a memorandum of understanding with Pradan. "Will the council funds be diverted to Pradan if the council signs this MoU with Pradan?" queried one member.

Another member asked, "How does the council benefit by signing this MoU?"

Kamakhya Singh and Zanid started taking every question in turn. As the discussion progressed, the ward members began to be convinced and finally agreed to enter into the agreement. This was the first time the council had ever signed a formal agreement with another organisation. Again, Kamakhya Singh was overcome with optimism. After signing the contract, Panchayat Bhawan opened six days a week, and executive committee members started meeting on the 7th of every month.

After more discussions with Pradan professionals, the executive members, including Kamakhya Singh, realised they were not doing enough despite the many opportunities. Once this realisation struck, all the ward members became active in no time. New notice boards, posters showing different activities of the village council, and a complaint box were installed in the council office. Members started encouraging women to participate more and more in council work. Once again, Kamakhya became active.

Pradan organised a 7-day study visit to Kerala for Kamakhya Singh, Triveni Mahto (the deputy mukhiya), Ashok Rana (a council member), and Munni *didi* and Sahodari *didi* from a women's group. The entire team was amazed to see the roles and changes brought about by the many village councils in Kerala.

"In Kerala, village-based women's groups have ensured food and nutritional security. Further, the council provided excellent education, drinking water, and health care services", commented Munni *didi*.

Kamakhya Singh was impressed by the active participation of the village communities and the feeling of ownership with their respective council. The visiting team experienced the potential of an empowered village council, the prospect of an empowered women's collective, and the possibility of a synergistic relationship between these two institutions. The team came back to Pindarkone with a different vision and a strong motivation.

A few days after the team's return, Pradan organised a 3-day 'visioning' workshop with community representatives, the women's group members, and community leaders under the leadership of Kamakhya Singh. Mr Singh could sense the positive energy and mutual trust among the executive members from the attendance and participation. He was convinced that the history of Pindarkone was going to be re-written. And when council members decided on the vision of their council – "*Hum gram panchayat ke pratinidhi evam janta; panchayat me addharbhut sanrachna, samjaik vikas, mahila sashaktikaran paryavaran evam rojgar ke liye pratibaddh hai.* (We, the representatives of the gram panchayat [the village council] and the people of Pindarkone, are committed to developing l ocal infrastructure, social development, women empowerment, environment protection, a nd employment generation)."

Kamakhya and Pradan representatives were happy. Zanid then added, "Kamakhya Sir, you are great; now, please identify the priorities for the council and start working." Three priority areas, namely education, employment (through agriculture and horticulture), and women empowerment, were identified for immediate attention.

After the workshop, Kanahya Singh held five executive committee meetings – more than what was mandatory – to discuss priorities and identify team leaders during the next month. He always made a point of inviting women leaders from the village. Dineshwar Ram and Lukeshwar Mahto were selected as 'ministers' for education and agriculture. The ministers selected the members for their committees in consultation with the council members.

Pradan trained them to prepare work plans and progress reports. Monthly meetings were planned for both committees. As Kamakhya realised that the ministers continued to depend on him even for minor decisions, he started withdrawing himself and compelling the committee members to make decisions on their own, based on what they had learnt during their training.

The committee led by the education minister, Dineshwar Ram, identified absenteeism and lack of punctuality among the teachers and lack of quality mid-day meals as the critical problems for schools. The minister decided to form a school management committee, with all the schools' principals or headteachers as members. At the village level, he also formed committees of children.

"Initially, a few people laughed at our committee and said that neither the teachers were going to change, nor the children would ever go to school", said Ramnarayan, a headteacher in one of the schools. He continued to inform, "We started holding village-level meetings with parents and working on infrastructure including toilets and drinking water supply in every school."

The parents and the children seemed happy. However, some headteachers refused to attend the meetings and tried to dissuade others from attending. They were against Kamakhya Singh and the education minister Dinesh Ram because the teachers did not want the village council to monitor their schools. They opposed the meetings and used the block- level teachers' association to oppose the council's decisions.

Dinesh Ram, finding no solution to overcome this resistance by the teachers, reached out to Kamakhya Singh. Together, they decided to appeal to the villagers and requested them to contact the headteachers of the respective schools. The villagers informed Singh that only five out of the forty-odd teachers opposed the idea. Both Singh and Ram visited a few schools to find out the problems faced by the teachers, who readily listed their grievances and difficulties. The significant issues highlighted were the lack of clean drinking water, washbasins, and separate toilets for girls. The council lost no time setting up the required facilities on the school premises under the guidance of Dinesh, the minister of education. Gradually, the trust between the council, parents, and teachers started getting more robust, and headteachers who had once been opposing the council began to support it.

All the executive members were pleasantly surprised when two children, Lalita and Bittu, the members of the children's committee, reported that the mid-day meals served in schools contained worms and that their teachers were always on the phone even during working hours. Both the mukhiya and the minister treated these complaints seriously and discussed the children's concerns with the core committee members. The results were quick, and the children were happy with improved food quality and their teachers. As the core committee started meeting more frequently, topics like school curriculum, lesson plans, and the pattern for marking and evaluation of students became part of the agenda. Sports, cultural programmes and various academic competitions were introduced in schools. Attendance increased as parents began insisting that their children attend school regularly. Kamakhya Singh was happy to observe a systemic change in the overall scenario of education.

Subsequently, the council built a library for children with the help of donations. A system of identifying outstanding teachers and students and rewarding them was established. Schools had become happening places with more and more children joining and teachers becoming regular.

"Have you noticed that now we have more than 20 per cent of students from those families who had never sent their children to school before?" asked Shiva of Pradan. And when Pindarkone received the 'Deen Dayal Upadhyaya Gram Panchayat Empowerment Award' for 2019-20 from the Government of India for its excellent work in education, the entire council celebrated the news with pride.

Farming was the only option for livelihood for most people in the villages under the panchayat—and they continued to farm traditionally, more for subsistence than for business. Lukeswar Mahato, the council minister for agriculture, voiced his lament thus: "We have received no help from the government. In the rainy season, water from the Barakar floods our villages: in summers, the wells and hand pumps go dry, and people have to walk up to two kilometres for water."

Based on his experience, Kamakhya Singh requested Pradan to arrange a study visit for the representatives of the village council to a successful watershed area. On their return, Kamakhya Singh and Lukeswar Mahato, who were part of the visiting team, led a meeting   of the members of the executive committee and the women's group and chalked out a detailed strategy for the overall development panchayat.

The committee, led by the minister, vowed to take the work forward. However, Lukeswar Mahato conceded, "We did not know how to move forward. We were told about 'convergence', but we didn't know what and how to go about it."

Kamakhya Singh, members of the committee, and two representatives of Pradan visited the office of the commissioner, North Chotanagpur and explained their plan. They requested her to call a meeting of all the state departments and agencies responsible for development.

In the meeting, the commissioner appreciated the activities of the village councils and instructed the officials to make the convergence plan part of the *'Adarsh gram panchayat'* (model village council) scheme.

"This meeting proved to be a milestone in developing the

Pindarkone village council", said Kamakhya Singh. He added, "Increasing water availability and irrigation facilities for the farmers were our primary objectives. State departments such as the Minor Irrigation Department created necessary infrastructures like check-dams and ponds and funded an electric sub-station. Creating water-conserving structures under MGNREGA (the central government's employment guarantee scheme) had duel benefits for us. We not only got wages but also created a network of irrigation channels in our villages."

The panchayat was now on the development radar of all the state departments and agencies. Infrastructure such as a local market came up within the council building in the village. The village council also organised training on agriculture and dairying for all villagers. Seven hundred farm families got their Kisan credit card (a credit card for farmers) and *fasal bima yojana* (crop insurance scheme).

"A lot has changed in our panchayat. Our village is becoming greener day by day, and people have new employment opportunities. This gives us a lot of satisfaction, " informed the proud Mukhiya Ji. Kamakhya Singh understood that one should dream and see dreams come true; one should be persistent in one's efforts and ready to face challenges.

The increased activities of the council inspired many women in the village, and their self- help groups became active quickly.

"I wanted something like a common services centre in the village, and while discussing the idea, we came up with the concept of a gram panchayat help desk. Two of the active members of the self-help group, Ruby *didi* and Munni *didi*, came forward to work at the help desk. With only two days of training, they learnt the ropes and knew what was expected of them", said Kamakhya Singh.

The help desk not only identified the poor and vulnerable households within the council's jurisdiction but also supported them in getting such essential documents as birth or death certificates, a certificate of income, and the Aadhar card (a national identity card). The help desk also helped the households apply for labour cards and pension schemes meant for the older people, widows, and differently-abled persons and submit the applications to the council office. As a result, more than 1200 vulnerable individuals were registered with the various development schemes of the government.

"All this was achieved through dedicated efforts by the help desk and members of self-help groups", Mr Singh announced with pride.

Afterword

Pindarkone was one of the 16 village councils in Jharkhand in which Pradan and Anode Governance Lab had launched their panchayat empowerment campaign.

"Although every panchayat has its own success story, Kamakhya Singh's Pindarkone was ahead of all others. It is an astounding success story where we not only satisfied all the technical indicators but also achieved more than what was expected socially," declared Shiva, who had been part of the campaign from the beginning. Zanid supported him by adding, "Kamakhya sir was a successful leader who just needed self-confidence and outside support. We have seen many well-begun and motivated efforts peter out, but, in this case, fortunately, Kamakhya's comeback made all the difference."

No doubt, many more challenges are still to be overcome. Nevertheless, team Pradan seemed confident that Kamakhya Singh, working in unison with his fellow council members, would overcome all the obstacles. "The Pinderkone village council has already become a model council, and Kamakhya Singh is now an inspiration to many community leaders", said a beaming Zanid.

When asked about his journey, the mukhiya Ji answered humbly: *"Haan, dusre janam mein kuch kamyabi to mili hai par rasta abhi lamba hai."* (Yes, in second birth I have had some successes, but I have a long way to go yet).

*****

Smaller Steps of Bigger Impacts
(Pradeep Kumar Mishra & Sasanka Shekhar Sahoo)

"The success did blind us to some extent. Our teachers also told us that taking community for granted is a rubric of failure, but we sometimes ignore it."

The story begins...

When Mr Sasanka, an MBA by training, joined the Koraput, Odisha team of Pradan, he was amazed to see the contradictions. A native of Bangurupada village, located in the denuded hills of Lamtaput block only 75 kilometres from the district headquarters, was resourceful, and there was no shortage of quality natural resources; still, the villagers were languishing in poverty. Though, in the past, his colleague, Samir, had taken a few initiatives in the villages to bring villagers out of poverty. Unfortunately, the task remained incomplete.

Bangurupada is a tribal village of 60 households dominated by the members of the *Gadaba* tribe, followed by the *Dama* community (scheduled caste) and Rana (other backward castes), respectively. The village on a hillock and surrounded by mountains presented a panoramic view. A small seasonal waterfall came alive during the rainy season, and the whole area turned into a green and clean artefact of nature.

Rainfed agriculture was the mainstay of the village. The landholding ranged from two to five acres. Villagers cultivated crops like paddy and millet for self-consumption.

"We have no other source of income, and because of the scarcity of water, we are not able to cultivate vegetables which may give us some extra income. Many of our young men and women migrate to other states – particularly to Andhra and Kerala in search of labour works", said Mr Dulhat bhaina a villager in his 50s.

Though Sasanka was aware of various successful projects that his organisation Pradan, had implemented in a few other villages, he knew that replicating a successful model of one village in another village is not a sure recipe for success.

"We decided to move forward with the community members so that change is neither drastic nor threatening", said Sasanka.

"Excellent, but can you explain a bit more to me?" I requested Sasanka.

"What I mean by drastic is just or almost opposite of their existing practices, and threatening is when community members think that the suggested strategies are against their culture and destroying their traditional knowledge", was the quick response of Sasanka.

Though villagers were engaged in organic cultivation, yield and return from their agriculture were limited.

"Though they followed organic agriculture, it was not scientific at all. People would throw the cow dung directly into the fields without processing it, expecting to increase their yield. The concept of composting[2] was still alien to them. And we knew that simply telling them will either not work at all, or if it works, it will take a very long time", shared Sasanka.

After a series of meetings informing villagers about the process and the importance of composting, fifty compost pits were constructed at the homestead lands of selected villagers by the team Pradan. Villagers, though not entirely convinced, participated mainly to see the outcome.

"Though we have heard about *Handi Khad, Jibamrita, Agneystra,* we didn't know and had not seen it. So when Sasanka bhaiya told us and showed us, we decided to use it in our fields," said Mr Bindhya, who had two compost pits in his backyard.

"Fortunately, the result was perfect and visible, and the weather also supported us. Yields went up considerably for all the villagers who used our recommendations. Now I was convinced that the practice of composting will spread faster," said Mr Ashok, a member of team Sasanka.

Success made Sasanka and his team impulsive, and they thought of bringing other changes faster. Next on their agenda was the introduction of the system of rice intensification (SRI) and the system of millet intensification (SMI) in their cultivation practices. They thought that as their first interventions had been successful and villagers had already tasted benefits,they would quickly adapt their subsequent recommendations. But unfortunately, only three families experimented with the suggestions. They were surprised and unable to find out what went wrong and why their recommendations were ignored?

Sasanka recalled, "we committed the same mistake I had warned my team. The success did blind us to some extent. Our teachers had also told us that taking community for granted is a rubric of failure, but we sometimes ignore it. We learnt the lesson soon, but of course, in a hard way," were the frank submission of Sasanka.

Villagers, particularly women who spent more time in the field than their male counterparts, considered it more time and resource consuming and said that the suggested farming system was unheard of and not tested. For almost all the villagers, practices like SRI and SMI were new and considering their economic status, it was wrong to expect that they would adopt any new system unless they were fully convinced.

Jaya Bhaina, whose wife was the Sarpanch, followed SRI practice on a small piece of his land. After seeing vigorous crops, he was angry with his fellow villagers. He even conveyed his anger to Shashanka, "sir, no one can change them, they deserve to be poor and remain poor. Please stop thinking for them".

The team was concerned but determined to continue introducing scientifically proven technologies. A meeting of the entire team

---

2. decomposing animal and plant wastes following a scientific process. The resulting mixture is rich in plant nutrients and beneficial organisms and increases soil fertility.

was called. After prolonged discussion, it was finalised that they would revert their strategy from introducing the technology first and then convincing the community to convince the community first and then requesting them to adopt it in a phased manner.

The team leader Shasanka, however, was in a hurry. "Can we find some successful examples where these farmers will get an exposure to similar interventions and start appreciating the possible benefits" asked Sasanka. He continued to add, "awareness, education and finally winning their confidence may take a long time for such technological interventions".

Sasanka, "can we consider Chhapuram village of Koraput district where farmers are of more or less similar socio-economic status and have started earning an additional income of up to 1 lakh annually because of adoption of better technologies"? Asked Rashmita, a senior colleague of Sasanka, who had visited the village once along with her team members almost six months back. After thinking for some time, Sasanka said, "Good idea. How didn't it occur to me? let's go, Chhapuram".

And the team proved correct. The farmers of Banguraupad were pleasantly surprised to see the development in village Chhapuram. Host villagers, too, seemed happy to know that people from nearby districts were visiting to learn about their works. They talked about *"nayi taknik* (new technology)" and the power of the community decision making process. After they returned to their village, Sasanka and the team arranged small video films dubbed in the local language related to SRI, SMI, and horticulture.

"These two interventions seemed working; villagers started discussing the modern techniques and also need of collaborative efforts by the villagers", informed Rashmita.

"The field demonstrations of improved techniques were taken seriously. Farmers participated and asked questions. Come next year, farmers started experimenting with SRI and SMI. The outcome of their experiments was encouraging, and then their faith in 'new technology' increased. Though it took two seasons, attitude and farming practices changed for the better," said Sasanka.

Unfortunately, the saying *Man proposes, God disposes* came true for Sasanka and his team. The following year turned out to be a dry year, and as expected, farmers started raising a hue and cry. After all, they had invested money, and they had very high expectations.

Sensing the gravity of the situation, Rashmita opened up, "we have to work very hard to keep the temper in control. Let's take the community along and address the issue once and for all".

Sasanka agreed but had a concern. "A permanent resolution will be costly. We need water for all seasons and all". And, we don't have money," said Sasanka.

"We should go and meet the district collector and explain the real situation. After all, villagers can't do everything," advised Rashmita.

"Done. Thank you. Let me test myself" said Sasanka.

Within two months, Sasanka, with the help of officers from the government department of horticulture, could impress the state-run Odisha Lift Irrigation Corporation (OLIC) to establish a lift irrigation facility in the village. Community members and Pradan shared some costs.

"The most encouraging experience I had was when villagers themselves said they would work jointly to manage the irrigation facilities. The visit to Chhapuram village proved useful", commented Sashak.

The villagers had started getting a better return from agriculture. But villagers were still not out of poverty and needed some additional support. After the team realised that villagers had begun aspiring for a better life and had displayed their collaborative skills, it would be fitting to look for ongoing government-sponsored schemes. Though Sasanka was aware of all those schemes, he encouraged the active members of the village to talk to the village Sarpanch.

The Village Sarpanch had a cautious reply, "government has enough schemes for the benefit of people. However, because there is no awareness and lack of teamwork and coordination at the village level, these benefits do not reach the villagers".

Sasanka, who had depended on his team and active villagers, decided to pass on the responsibility to the women representatives of selected SHGs to coordinate different schemes. Sarpanch, too, became involved and joined villagers in visiting officers of various departments. Slowly, external bits of help started tickling. Though it was not much, it added to the villagers' cheerful disposition and enthusiasm.

Three years have passed. Both village and villagers have transformed. The village is greener, and with more activities across the year, villagers are happier, satisfied, united, and connected. New farming techniques have reduced the labour work. Production of paddy and millets has gone up. Farmers have started vegetable cultivation for commercial purposes. The total area under cultivation has gone up from five to thirty acres.

"Today in Lamtaput market, everyone talks about our village because we are the major source of watermelon in the local market," said Phulmati, a proud watermelon grower.

The selling price too increased, and farmers were making a profit. "This year, I sold watermelon for sixty thousand rupees. Initially, I was the only person from our group who cultivated watermelon. Now everyone does it," informed Bhanu Khilo'.

Increased production, increased income, and ambition to grow created a market for new products and services in the local area.

"I was knowing it that farmers will look for quality seeds, organic fertilisers, and technologies. I identified a few young boys and encouraged them to plunge into business. Two of them agreed and became agriculture entrepreneurs and are doing well. We helped both get both technical and financial support from the state-run agency Agriculture Promotion and Investment Corporation of Odisha Limited".

Young entrepreneurs were putting their blood and sweat into business. Regular interactions with customers, packaging products as per the requirements of individual farmers, linking them with the buyers of their products who offered reasonable prices, and charging negligible for their services were mantras they followed.

"I help my fellow villagers by providing quality inputs, aggregating their produce, and facilitating sale at a reasonable price, " informed Raghunath Krisani, a class 8th pass young entrepreneur. He earned about fifty thousand rupees as a commission from the service provided to the villagers.

Smaller land holdings, smaller marketable surplus, lack of negotiation skills and power, and need for fast cash were still limiting farmers' income. Villagers were finding it challenging to invest both in cultivation and marketing.

"Though villagers were not much aware of the concept of producer group (PG), we formed a group to strengthen the villagers' marketing activities. Considering the ability to scale up the producer group's operation, we decided to keep membership open for the villagers of two adjoining villages, namely, Raipada and Bandhapada," said Sasanka. With 149 members, the PG, namely, Jai Jagannath Producer Group, engaged in bulk marketing.

"We started getting seeds at 20% lower price, and our marketing cost reduced significantly. As buyers started visiting us in the village, we felt comfortable and could negotiate good prices for our products. Also, no more distress selling for us. During the last Kharif season, our group supplied one truckload of vegetables every week to the market," informed Mr Brahmesh, one of the young farmers of village Raipada. Subsistence farming was wholly replaced by commercial agriculture with an average increase in annual income rupees eighty thousand rupees for the framers of village Bangurupada.

Bangurupada has changed. Greenery, which was limited to the rainy season, was now a year-long feature of the village. Denuded hillocks had natural vegetation making them green, and the waterfall is seen throughout the year except in three summer months. Even with smaller land holdings, farmers made profits up to one lakh every year. A village that was not even on the map of government agencies was the favourite model village of almost all the government departments. Though social hierarchy had not yet diminished, the boundaries have blurred. A rare example of successful development intervention in which the community moved up on the ladder of empowerment and prosperity by taking one step at a time.

It was still a story in the making. Villagers had just learnt the business. In years to come, these villagers can become the hub of vegetable marketing. They were jointly deciding what crop farmers would grow.

"I don't know how long I will continue, but this story will become stronger and more interesting for many who doubt the power of the poor. They take smaller steps, but the impact of each step is bigger and cumulative," concluded Sasanka.

*****

Solar Power: Lighting up Countless Lives
(Balram Bhushan & Arpan Oraon)

*"It was common for us to find dogs and cats in and near our beds.
Snakes and rats crawling across legs were normal. Thanks to
the blessings of Suryadev, we now have some
light in our lives."*

The story begins...

I was exhausted after completing a session on sustainable energy for the representatives of Indian Non-Government Organizations. At the end of my session, one of the participants asked, "Have you ever seen solar energy as a means of sustainable livelihood and a happy lifestyle? We use it because we don't have any other option. It is still one of the costlier sources of energy. Sir, how do you justify the fact that while we force villagers to dole out almost 10% of their total earnings to meet their energy needs, all of us comparatively more affluent people do not spend even 2%?"

Those were the hard-hitting words, which forced me to think. Sustainable energy sources are meaningful only if they make life better and empower the user reasonably. I decided to explore a place, where solar power has truly transformed people's lives without costing much. I contacted my friend Arpan Oraon. He was working with an organisation called Pradan. This organisation has a history of implementing multiple innovative solutions to empower rural communities. I asked, "Do you have a true success story related to the use of solar power?"

He answered cleverly, "Yes, we have one project in the Gumla district of Jharkhand. Instead of judging it as being successful or otherwise, we

do what we believe will help the community. But yes, we have been able to fulfil many villagers' dreams of seeing electricity in their own houses and village."

We talked over the phone and decided it would be better to meet in person and learn about the project in detail. But the question that the participant had asked me remained at the top of my mind. I couldn't resist and asked, "Is it justifiable that we take the solar route to electricity though it is costlier and cumbersome?"

Arpan replied with the same composure, "Sometimes numbers are scarier than reality. We don't calculate cost when related to their survival, happiness, and hope. We believe that any interventions that bring smiles and satisfaction are worth trying out."

Though it was a wise answer, I was still not convinced. I requested a field visit to this site. He replied, "Join me in the first week of the next month when I have a scheduled visit to the village".

As I have the habit of viewing reality through written words, I started studying the bright side of Indian nights through some current but authentic publications. The official information was impressive. One could have quickly concluded that there was no need for sustainable energy. As per the information provided by government sources, in June 2021, rural India received an average electricity supply of over 22 hours per day, and for cities, the number was above 23 hours.

Are lanterns now antique? No, not at all! Not all the villages and households are fully electrified, nor is 24X7 electric supply a reality.

Further, widely dispersed and remote villages and lack of regular services and maintenance make solar one of the most viable electricity options in such situations. Undoubtedly, the government is trying its best to ensure electricity in every house in the country. Still, it will take a few more years to electrify all the villages and hamlets fully.

I was waiting for Arpan at the Gumla bus stand. As soon as he arrived, we started for Bhinjpur on his bike. He told me that the quality of the roads was terrible. In fact, after a few kilometres, there was no road at all. It was a challenging pillion-riding experience for me to reach Bhinjpur, a settlement of 115 families in Rajma village of Kobja panchayat. After arriving at Bhinjpur, I was introduced to Pramila Devi and Saraswati Devi.

When Arpan informed them about my interest in the solar project, Saraswati Devi began narrating her side of the story. "Since our childhood, nights meant darkness, and lanterns were our lifelines. We considered electricity a luxury, which could only be accessed by rich people and those who lived in cities," said Saraswati.

She had just finished when Pramila started talking, "It was common for us to find dogs and cats in and near our beds. Snakes and rats crawling across their legs were normal for those who slept on the ground. Thanks to the blessings of Suryadev (the Sun god), we now have some light in our lives too."

"Earlier, our life revolved around sunlight — we got up early in the morning, worked till dusk, had dinner and went to bed as soon as it was dark. I know an old lady who had dreamt of seeing electricity before her death," added Saraswati.

It was not even an hour since I had reached the village; I could decipher that the entire conversation revolved around darkness and obscurity. "Who are these outspoken ladies?" I asked.

Mr Arpan replied, "These are women from the village. More specifically, they are representatives of a women's federation — a collective (SHG/self-help group) formed with the help of an organisation named Pradan."

I was taken to the house of Mr Drigpal Singh. Seeing Arpan, a couple of villagers also joined us. Drigpal had a pucca house, although most walls lacked plastering. "Sir, ever since I found a krait (a venomous snake) between my legs, I stopped sleeping on the floor. It is only for the last few months after we got solar electricity that I have again started sleeping on the floor."

I asked Drigpal, "Have you ever tried to get electricity through the government channels?"

He smiled and said, "Even today, we are trying. People tried a lot; we approached every authority, individual, and organisation we felt could help. We discussed the issue several times in the Gram

Sabha and asked the Panchayat President to take the initiative for village electrification. The Gram Sabha representatives approached the Block Development Officer, but nothing happened. We also organised an event in the village and invited the MLA and the MP. They did make promises, but as you see, the village is yet to get electricity. Finally, Arpan bhaiya brought us light."

I was about to ask about the beginning of the solar movement in the village. At that point, Arpan introduced me to another gentleman, Krishna Singh, and told me he would brief me about the solar story of the village.

"Sir, this village never had an electricity connection, and we were born and brought up in the light of lanterns. However, when I visited Rajasthan for work, I saw solar-based systems used to charge mobile phones. After talking to those people, I realised that solar power could also be used in my house for lighting at night and playing amplifiers in the daytime. I learnt the technology from them and brought the entire system from Rajasthan. There were no bulbs compatible with the solar system; hence, I used a motor-vehicle bulb. It worked, and the villagers got some idea about solar power," explained Krishna Singh.

My opinion about the villagers changed completely. Krishna had turned out to be a smart villager, a perfect example of a 'jugaad' innovator.

However, the urge for electrification became more potent in 2015 when the villagers formed self-help groups (SHGs). Forming SHGs was the first intervention by Arpan. Within a few days, people started discussing the issues in the village and raising their concerns during meetings. During one of the discussions, Pramila didi spoke about Krishna Singh's successful experiment with solar energy and requested villagers to think of it and explore it further.

"I, too, had heard about Krishna Singh's tryst with solar power. But I was not sure about the technology. I used all my sources and Pradan's connections to gather information about any successful interventions using solar power for electricity", accepted Arpan.

Later on, a group of villagers (both men and women) went to Dariwadi, Maharastra, to see the successful model of a solar electrification project. After their return, during a specially convened Gram Sabha meeting, they were requested to share their experiences and opinions about whether the model would work in their context.

Most villagers did not show much interest in technical details during the meeting but were very enthusiastic about the electricity in their village. Surprisingly, almost everyone was able to catch the phrase "solar grid" and was using it quite frequently in their communication.

Arpan was clear that initial investments and technical requirements had to be arranged by Pradan. However, he decided to form an electrification committee with both women and men in a 60:40 ratio as its members. Villagers were requested to contribute their labour for free, and SHGs were asked to prepare a roster of workers so that no family would have all its members working to install the solar grid.

"The villagers were so enthusiastic about the project that when the work was allotted to one family member, other family members voluntarily joined the work. We found the villagers highly interested and attentive during their training on repairing and maintaining solar grids, microgrids, and other supporting systems. The SHGs decided to form another team by themselves to ensure timely collection of billed amounts from all the villagers," disclosed Arpan while explaining the installation process.

Villagers viewed the installation of this solar grid as the end of their perpetual darkness. Mrs Pramila said, "Arpan bhaiya personally helped the village solar electrification committee finalize the charges of electricity. The idea was to generate sufficient corpus for meeting all expenses, including operator fee, land lease, maintenance costs, and future expenses."

The final cost per household was Rupee 100.00 as fixed cost plus Rupee 20.00 per unit of electricity consumed.

"20 rupees per unit! It is very expensive. Are the villagers happy?" I asked.

Ms Saraswati replied, "It may be costly for you but not for us. We have seen those days of darkness, when watching television or using a mixer grinder was just wishful thinking. We are ready to pay even 20 rupees per unit, just for street lights, from our savings."

This was unimaginable for me, and hence I decided to stay in the village for a day and study the various usages of solar electricity. Pramila took me to the house of one Mrs Sohana. It was a semi-*pucca* house of two rooms. While we talked and had *sharbat* (lemonade), I could hear what sounded like a cricket commentary. I asked, "Who is inside?"

Mrs Sohana replied, "My son is a great fan of cricket, and he is watching a cricket match on TV. Thanks to Arpan *bhaiya*, my son is sitting here; otherwise, he would have gone to the local market and watched the match standing in front of a shop."

"So, people can even run TVs on solar power?" I asked Arpan.

Arpan replied, "People underestimate the sun's power. Apart from solar bulbs, televisions, mixers, small electronic gadgets, and even flour-mills run on solar power", said Arpan with a smile on his face and pride in his eyes.

I thought to myself, my monthly earnings may be more than the annual earnings of many of these villagers, and I pay less than 5 rupees per unit of electricity; still, my electricity bill hurts me. These people pay 20 rupees per unit, and still are happy. At that moment, I recalled the advice of my grandfather that happiness is a state of mind. If you choose to be satisfied, nothing can stop you.

With every meeting, my amazement and my curiosity went on increasing. I threw another question at Arpan, "See, establishing a solar grid is not a difficult task. Maintenance is the most critical issue. Many governmental initiatives targeted solar electrification of streets and roads, but most of them stopped working after a few months."

Calm Arpan was prepared with an answer, "Interventions fail when there is no ownership   by the user. In our case, there is 100% community ownership. We have a functional system of monthly bill collection that creates a corpus to take care of maintenance costs. A group of villagers is trained to deal with day-to-day maintenance, and we intervene if the matter is too technical."

Saraswati didi added, "However, I would agree that getting the unanimous support of the entire community was not easy, and we encountered unexpected hindrances. For example, when we were about to start the installation, a few villagers spreading the rumour, "Ye *jagah dev sthal hai, yahan solar grid baithane se gaon me kaal aa jayega* (if a solar grid is established on this sacred land, there would be calamities in the village)". Coincidently, within a fortnight, a kid's sudden demise occurred, and people started attributing the demise to the solar grid."

Arpan continued, "Although the incident created some hurdles, continuous persuasion, education and follow-up helped us overcome such challenges. Village leaders like Saraswati Devi, Pitambar Singh, and Pramila Devi have played significant roles in mobilising and convincing villagers. Frankly, it is the untiring efforts of such villagers that have changed people's lives."

Afterword

Frankly, all this seemed to be straight out of a fantasy film for me! When I got the opportunity to meet Mr Pitamber Singh, I said, "I just can't believe it, but all of you have worked a miracle in this village."

Mr Singh looked at me and said, "It sounds like a fairy tale, but we struggled very hard. In my entire life, I have never done something like this." Mobilising people and making them part of the change-making process was a challenging task for him. "But, yes, when we see the outcome today, those challenges appear small. For us villagers, solar energy is not only electricity but also a tool for revolutionising the entire society and economy," said a happy and contended Pitambar Singh. He took us to the house of Mrs Santoshi Devi.

Santoshi Devi's story was even more inspiring, "Earlier, we used diesel operated huller machines. When solar electrification came into the village, I thought of a rice hauling enterprise and invested 40000 to 45000 rupees to set up a rice hauling enterprise. By charging 1 rupee per kg for steamed paddy and 2 rupees for fresh paddy, I earn 1200 to 2600 rupees per day, depending upon the raw material I get."

"What is your net profit after paying the bill for solar electricity?" I asked.

"Around 10000 to 12000 rupees per month, after deduction of all maintenance costs and paying the electricity bill," was her simple answer.

"Since October 2020, there have been three huller machines in the village. Earlier, when there was only one, the waiting period for the villagers used to be a week. Now people get their rice hauled within a day using an excellent quality solar electricity-based hauling machine," informed Pitambar Singh.

Another solar energy-induced entrepreneur, Muni Devi, cultivated vegetables three cycles in a year — Kharif, Rabi and summer. Earlier, her income from selling vegetables was 400 rupees per week. Due to the availability of solar electricity, irrigating crops became effortless and cheaper. Now she earns 20000 rupees per year from the same land.

Solar electricity has also influenced the social interactions of the villagers. Mr Drigpal Singh said, "Earlier, people used to take dinner before sunset and sleep before dark. Now, people go to bed around 9 pm." He further added, "Earlier, when we talked to each other in the evenings, it was just words. Now, in addition to the words, we observe facial expressions and body language. Overall, our days have become longer, and we have blissful evenings."

"The government of India has decided to electrify every household of every village in the country. Now many villagers have both solar and usual connections. They are called 'double electricity supply' ", informed Arpan.

I asked Mrs Saraswati, "Why didn't you wait to get cheap

electricity through the electricity board instead of high-cost solar electricity?" She laughed and said, "It is good that solar power came before electrification by the government. Solar is always good. Who will give you electricity 24 hours a day? It is possible only through solar power."

By then, I was fully convinced about the power of solar power and how it had changed villagers' lives.

"Will you keep using solar power even after getting the electricity supply from the electricity board?" was my last question.

Mr Pitamber Singh and Mrs Saraswati replied with a loud "Yes".

Mr Pitamber Singh added, "We have already made all arrangements for keeping solar power alive...Now villagers want even solar-powered streetlights. We will study the feasibility of that as well."

It was late evening. All the houses were lit with solar lights.

Arpan wanted to stay in the village for a while. But I remembered the road condition and wanted to return a bit early. As I was about to mount his bike, he asked me, "What do you now think about solar energy?"

I replied, "It is magnificently fantastic! Hats off to you and the incredible technology. Thank you, Arpan bhaiya."

*****

From Suffering to Bliss: A Tale of Rajpur

(Satyendra Nath Mishra & Mohini Saha)

"The best thing that happened to me was that I could see an increase in women's self-esteem, being respected by others, and the financial stability of almost all the villagers."

The story begins...

Mohini, born and brought up in a city, was mesmerised by the pristine and natural landscape of the village and its surroundings. The bright sunshine on lush green fields, scurrying squirrels, chirping birds, crowing roosters, stars twinkling in the clear night sky, and the simplicity of the people of Rajpur enchanted her.

Rajpur village is situated in Narharpur block in the state of Chhattisgarh. The village is about 35 kms from Kanker, the district headquarters. The Gonds, one of the primitive tribes of India, were the native inhabitants of this village and constituted 91 per cent of the total population. Gonds are known for their unique culture, language, and forest-dependent lifestyle. The villagers mostly speak the Chhattisgarhi dialect. Their festivals, such as *Pola* and *Hareli*, are related to their continuing cultural association with forests, agriculture, and cattle. Their culture and social practices have ensured the conservation of available resources and sustained the productivity of land and cattle. The younger generations also celebrate the festivals of *Karwa Chauth, Navratri,* and *Ganesh Chaturthi.*

Mohini considered herself fortunate to have joined Pradan, as a development apprentice in Rajpur. Rani didi, who had become a good

friend of Mohini, told her that they were learning and imbibing new cultural practices due to migration and access to television and mobiles. When Mohini interacted with Devkunwar didi, she joyfully recalled, "In our culture, no festival is possible without mahua (a local home-brewed toddy)." Mohini was surprised at how the village culture had given space to women to enjoy the celebrations by partaking of local alcoholic drinks.

It was one of the early days of Mohini's apprenticeship. She was walking down the muddy lanes of Rajpur with Shivlal, a young and active villager. "*Bhaiya,* can you tell me about the history of this village?" asked Mohini.

Shivlal had found her sincere in her work and interested in learning, and hence decided to give a detailed reply. He started by mentioning, "We have heard from our elders that over 100 years ago, those who worked for the local king were given lands to settle here. Therefore, the village is named Rajpur." He continued to explain the village's history, but his voice changed when he mentioned, "Until a few years back, we, the men of this village, used to go to nearby villages along with our family members to work on the lands of large farmers. We did not have any work in the village, and the land we owned was not enough to meet our needs."

Mohini learned that big farmers from nearby villages used to come with their vehicles to take villagers from Rajpur for manual labour. Borrowing money from moneylenders was common, and some of the villagers had forfeited their lands as they could not repay their loans.

Mehtarin daai ('daai' is grandmother in the local language), even at the age of 90, knitted brooms to survive. The condition in which she lived and the stories she shared gave Mohini an idea of what the villagers had endured for the last six decades. She remembered daai saying, "When I came to the village after my marriage, we did not have even rice to eat." Mohini was at a loss for words.

Although Mohini had completed just one month, she could sense that the villagers lived with a sense of insecurity. Unsure of their income, they did not know how they would be able to get a square meal the next day. Complete dependence on the rains for agriculture had made their farming unpredictable and unremunerative.

Dhruv Saroj, who owned three acres of land, said, "My agriculture is dependent on rainfall. I was often unable to recover my investments, which is true for almost everyone in the village".

Most of the land was undulating. During rains, the runoff caused topsoil erosion and damaged the crops in the lower lands because of the high velocity of water and the flood- like situation. Even in the best years, villagers could cultivate vegetables, maize, and pulses on their uplands and paddy in mid and lowlands during the Kharif season (June to October) because of the limited availability of moisture in the soil. For the rest of the year, land remained uncultivated. Even the wells ran dry due to the decreasing groundwater levels.

Mohini was worried about the prevailing conditions of vulnerability, poverty, and food insecurity. Women and children were the worst sufferers. Sunita didi shared, "In our society, women eat last at home and don't get sufficient food, and we can't do anything in this regard.

Speaking out about our plight is not looked at favorably in our society."

The villagers had gotten some relief with the implementation of the government's Mahatma Gandhi National Rural Employment Guarantee Act (MGNREGA) program. However, though the program guaranteed 100 days of employment, getting even 90 days of employment was rare. Only one person per household was permitted to seek work under this scheme.

Further, most of the villagers were unaware of the role of the Gram Sabha (village level institutions) in preparing the labour budget under the MGNREGA. Arjun Komra shared his pain, "Farmers used to submit requests for farm bunding or farm ponds on their land, but these remained pending for months, and most of the time, they did not materialise." Though a few farm ponds were created in the village, all of those were near the fields of selected influential farmers.

"No doubt, after the inception of MGNREGA, there was some relief, and people began to get work. The seasonal migration was also reduced to some extent. However, the overall condition of the village and villagers remained uncertain and distressing," Shivlal bhaiya recalled.

During 2009-10, a few farmers started growing hybrid paddy using chemical fertilisers. However, it was expensive. Mohini realised that though hybrid paddy had higher production, this could turn into a debt trap for farmers in case of weather aberration.

At the same time, three women's self-help groups (SHGs) were formed in the village. Women who were members used to meet once a month and deposit Rupee 5.00 per month per member. Their only objective was to save money. Sunita didi shared, "We used to go for the meeting, deposit five rupees and return."

"This is not development. Development does not happen in bits and pieces," Mohini told herself. She seemed concerned but felt helpless. She decided to convey the same to the state head office of Pradan.

Masroor, an experienced professional at Pradan, who had earlier worked in the area, had a detailed conversation with Mohini. Mohini respected him as a passionate development professional with a lot of experience working in diverse conditions. Mohini shared her opinion during the discussion, "Sir, I see that the villagers are under severe economic stress, and they have some genuine problems; however, they are still not opening up, and I am not sure how to help them."

After listening to Mohini, Masroor smiled as if he was expecting it. He answered, "Initially, I too had a similar feeling. I felt like an outsider, and community members also felt the same. However, over some time, when you start recognising their concerns empathetically and acknowledge the same, they will open up to you. They will start looking at you as an individual, who knows them well and is there to help them out."

At the end of their lengthy discussion, Mohini appeared happy and satisfied. "Thank you very much, sir. You have compelling ideas, and I shall start working on them right away," were Mohini's parting comments.

Mohini was on her mission. It was the beginning of 2011, and changes in the village of Rajpur were evident. SHGs and their meetings, which were hitherto only a means of monthly saving by the women, started exploring possibilities of taking some concrete action as a collective. Training sessions were organised for the executives and general members. Though the process was slow, the change in attitude was visible. In less than eight months, there were nine functional SHGs. Women of every household, including the most vulnerable and ultra- poor, had become SHG members.

All the SHGs came together to create a village organisation (VO). The VO was visualised as a platform for linking government programs and pooling resources for village upliftment. Now Mohini was in action.

Food security and income enhancement of the villagers were Mohini's new areas of focus. Mohini was aware that villagers had lands, but their productivity was too low because of the lack of proper irrigation facilities. She knew that waiting or working for irrigation facilities for the villagers was not a rational option, so she consulted her colleagues for various economically feasible alternatives. Over the next few months, demonstrations of improved techniques in water-stressed agriculture were organised. Women were provided with field- level training in the System of Rice Intensification (SRI), a method wherein less seed and less water are used to obtain higher production. They were also provided with input-based support to try out the new technique.

Ganga *didi* was the first to try out SRI. Her fellow villagers, including her family members, laughed at her, wondering how two kgs of seed could be sufficient when the usual requirement was 20 kgs. Using just one paddy seedling per clump was beyond the villagers' imagination. However, the mocking farmers were shocked to see the status of Ganga didi's field. Her plants were greener, more vigorous and had ears full of grains. Her total production of 21 quintals of paddy in one acre of land was double the average production. Now it was Ganga didi's turn to smile.

Mohini could experience the increased confidence and trust of the villagers in her. She acknowledged, "It was Pradan's success, and I must say Masroor Sir's suggestions were the turning point in the story of Rajpur."

Looking at the increasing activities of the SHGs and women members' interest in agriculture, Mohini had an idea to test. She decided to combine the efforts for SHGs' empowerment and agricultural promotion. She requested women SHG leaders of Rajpur to plan their agricultural activities during SHG meetings. During these meetings, mutual discussions helped individual members plan their farming based on their knowledge and experience. Training in collective agriculture helped members enhance their understanding of scientific agriculture and convince their family members to adopt it.

"We did not even know how much land we owned, which seed to sow, or the names of fertilisers or pesticides. Once we started planning in our SHGs and attending training sessions, we started learning everything", shares Ganga *didi*.

Although all the SHGs were on the move, the Ugta Suraj SHG, under the leadership of Rajo *didi*, Sunita *didi*, and Ganga *didi*, became the catalyst of change in Rajpur and the neighbouring villages of Masulpani, Dabena, and Devgaon also.

For Mohini, Hemlata *didi*, a native of Rajpur, was the epitome of women's empowerment. Within a couple of years of her marriage, her husband had started harassing and humiliating her. She joined the Ugta Suraj SHG. With the help of her SHG sisters, she raised her voice against the injustice she suffered in her family. She fought for women's rights within the family and the village. It was primarily through her efforts that SHGs gained considerable say in village-level decision making. She was now the role model for many of the villagers.

By the beginning of 2014, sixty-five women SHGs, with 750 members, were active in the villages of Masulpani, Dabena and Devgaon. To ensure practical learning, field visits to Rajnagar were conducted, and members were exposed to the new agricultural practices and the role of collectives.

Ganga *didi* recalled, "To celebrate our unity, togetherness, and strength, we organised cluster *adhiveshan* (meeting). In addition to sharing our experiences, we carried out rallies to raise awareness, sang motivational songs, and even played kabaddi together. What a joy it was!"

However, the joy was short-lived for villagers. In June 2013, there was good rainfall. Farmers were busy preparing their lands for various crops. But unfortunately, in July, when usually a good rain was expected, there was no rain at all. The sowing of different crops, including paddy and vegetables, was severely affected. The mood got sullen, and everyone, including Mohini, felt helpless. Ashutosh, a colleague of Mohini who had recently joined Pradan, was in the line of fire. The villagers started complaining that he had taken only half-steps and had not planned for such weather aberrations.

Over the next two months, consultations with the villagers of all four villages made the team Mohini realise the urgent need for harnessing water resources. Mohini was convinced of the competency of women-led SHGs and decided to engage them in creating awareness for integrated natural resource management (INRM) practices. Mohini and Ashutosh joined hands to explain the need for and the process of INRM. The idea was to develop community- owned INRM assets, such as farm ponds, smaller water storage structures, and farm bunding. The villagers did not take much time to say 'yes'.

However, the common concern for most villagers was that, if they created small ponds in their fields, there would be lesser space for them to cultivate crops. Several villagers were apprehensive about converting 20 dismal (about 20 square feet) of land into a rainwater harvesting structure. For the villagers, the land was not just a piece of soil but also a means of social recognition and the only assured source of their livelihood. Leaders of the Ugta Suraj SHG took the responsibility of convincing farmers. The Sarpanch of the Gram Panchayat (GP) and one of his close friends offered help to the SHG in mobilising villagers.

It took almost two months of continuous persuasion, including video shows and one-to-one meetings, to see some softening in villagers' stand. In one of the village meetings, Rajo *didi* asked Ashutosh, "So tell us, what needs to be constructed and where?"

Ashutosh had just started explaining when Mohini stopped him.

Mohini told villagers, "Let us meet tomorrow; we shall come

prepared to explain everything to you."

Mohini advised Ashutosh that they should stop giving suggestions to villagers, which was a top-down approach. Ashutosh got the message and nodded in agreement. During the next meeting with the SHG members, village elders, and farmers, Mohini and her team facilitated a social and resource mapping exercise. This visualisation exercise carried out by the team led everyone to appreciate the possible solutions. Mohini had mastered the art of presenting complex processes in simple words. The SHG members called the Patwari (government land records keeper) to share the map of the village and farmers' fields. This exercise led the villagers to identify different types of land, causes of water runoff, locations for effective water conservation, and sites for plantation.

Ganga *didi* recalls, "We divided our village into three parts. We physically visited each other's land and decided on places for water harvesting structures. Usually, we used to visit each other's fields for work, but visiting with a specific plan, as an expert, was a new experience and feeling for all of us."

Sunita *didi* remembers their next course of action, "We shared our plans in the Gram Sabha for the first time. More than 60 per cent of the women members participated. We finalised 29 farm ponds and ten farm bunds in the upland areas under MGNREGA.

Poultry sheds were planned for economically vulnerable families, whose landholdings were either too small or did not allow the construction of other structures. We organised a joint meeting with the MGNREGA cell officials and shared our plans. They were excited to see our plans, and our work started. It was our work, and we knew what we were doing and why."

Ashutosh was surprised by women members and their leaders. Though he was thrilled, he had not expected villagers to complete such technical tasks.

"Mohini, your coaching has worked. See the works of Sunita Didi and other women leaders; they have surprised everyone. I am pleased about it", told Ashutosh.

By 2018, the planned work was completed. During this period, the women's collective ensured the quality implementation of INRM. The idea of *Mang Patra was* a unique way of ensuring that all those who needed work and applied for it got the opportunity to work and wages. An equitable method of ensuring work according to villagers' demands under MGNREGA.

Happy Pilaram Komra informed, "I got both my farm ponds constructed. Now, whenever it doesn't rain, we use water from our pond to irrigate my paddy crop. In addition, for the last three years, I got the entire 150 days of work on my job card."

Mohini and villagers considered farm ponds to be a boon for the villagers. However, unfortunately, four out of every five ponds started drying up by December, after the first monsoon. As the villagers had tested the power of collectives and had developed complete faith in Mohini and her team, they sought her help in getting expert help.

Mohini organised a meeting with her senior colleagues having watershed management expertise. It was concluded that upland ponds would not be able to hold water if medium and lower areas were not treated with water-recharge interventions. Masroor, Mohini, and Ashutosh were closeted for a couple of hours to discuss this recommendation. However, the team was convinced that even the ongoing project would not succeed unless this were completed. They were also clear that they would not be able to meet the total cost required for the newly recommended activities. Masroor decided to take the help of a state-level team for this project. Convergence of other projects being implemented in the district was considered the most viable option to ensure the timely completion of the proposed task.

Mohini started meeting district heads of different state departments to explore the possibility of multi-agency collaboration. The women's group completed the resource mapping in the village, i.e., marking irrigated and unirrigated land patches, drainage lines flow, and other socio-economic details. Ashutosh ensured that community leaders completed all mapping and probable structures, water budgeting depicting water availability, cropping system and additional water requirement. Finally, the project was implemented with the help of the State MGNREGA Cell, Bharat Rural Livelihood Foundation, Pradan, State government agencies, and the collective efforts of villagers.

The proud and happy Sarpanch shares, "About 80 villagers took the transect walk together for four days to decide the locations of

39 farm ponds, 17 farm bunds, 12 pond de-silting works, and draining line treatment. And, once these were decided, completing them took less than six months."

Mohini's meetings with the representatives of different departments enabled the linking of numerous villagers with other ongoing projects, such as the provision of solar pumps by the government for selected farmers having ponds under *Saur Sujala Yojana*, bunding, levelling of fields, and training for cultivation of vegetables, pulses and millets by the State agriculture and horticulture departments. Further, families owning poultry sheds were linked with the state-run animal husbandry department under the *Backyard Kukkat Palan Ekaae*. Mohini ensured that villagers were trained enough to benefit from all the schemes.

Rajnagar changed, and villages nearby also changed. The paddy-only area grew vegetables, pulses, oilseeds, and wheat. Water was no longer a limitation. Sulochna Saroj, from Masulpani village, had many developments to share, "I own two acres of land. I have two farm ponds and one well dug under MGNREGA on my family's land. In 2020, I also got a solar pump set for a dug well. Today I rear fish in those ponds and produce a double crop of vegetables, pulses, oilseeds, and wheat. I do not eat fish, but my daughter loves to eat it, and I sell it to my fellow villagers. My life has changed for the better."

While talking to colleagues, Mohini shares that from 2019 onwards, the paddy productivity had increased from two to three tonnes. This was because of access to improved irrigation techniques and practices in paddy cultivation. A family engaged in fish farming earned an additional Rupee 15,000.00 per month. In the last few years, the annual income of 632 families has reached more than Rupee 1,00,000.00

Afterword

The success of Rajnagar and its three adjoining villages has encouraged other nearby villagers to explore and experiment with the idea of creating natural resource-based assets. As a result, Pradan, too, has planned to take its successful model to other villages.

Mohini now had many accomplishments to feel upbeat about. Three hundred and sixty individual farm ponds, levelling of 216 farm plots, and plantation work on 70 farmers' lands, saving more than 156-hectare meters of runoff, are no less than commendable successes. However, she is happier to have won the trust of the villagers. Most young villagers call her Mohini didi, and elders always respect her.

When asked about her apprenticeship, Mohini recalls, "The best thing that happened to me was that I could see an increase in women's self-esteem, being respected by others, and the financial stability of almost all the villagers."

Mohini, now a regular and confirmed professional of Pradan, is still interested in continuing her job in the same area. No doubt, there are new lucrative offers with hefty pay packages, but she has decided to continue with her existing organisation.

*****

Lifting Lives with Solar Lift
(Niraj Kumar & Amit Kumar Singh)

"I should confess that neither the terrain nor the people of Lalpur were new to me, but the solution had to be unique for both."

The story begins...

An old farmer looking up at a cloudy sky is probably the most common image of a typical Indian farmer. Although only an image, it says a lot about the status of farmers in India— but not to me it did not: when I found a group of farmers in Lalpur, a small village in the Dindori district of Madhya Pradesh, in that iconic pose, I wondered whether any film was being shot. However, their grim faces were telling something else.

"*kya baat hai, aap sab itne mayus kyun ho?* (What is the matter? Why are you all looking so dejected?)", I asked as I walked toward them and greeted them.

Bhagwati bai, who was one of the oldest but most vocal among them, replied, "*Ye pacchis metre ki duri marein ja rahi hai bhaiya* (Brother, this 25-metre strip is a matter of life and death for us!)," she replied as she stared at the river barely 25 metres away from their fields.

The farmers had tried to use locally available pumps and other traditional means to get the river water to their fields without success. The last time, Bhagwati bai's son Khem Singh had installed a brand-new pump – and had even performed a *pooja* before switching on the pump – but failed to irrigate his crops. The only option was to buy a bigger, more powerful pump— which was unaffordable. The farmers had pleaded with officials of the local government and even appealed to political leaders, but to no avail. After all, their number was too small to carry any administrative and political weight.

I remembered a very old number that my father frequently sang from the Hindi film *Amanush*: "*Sagar kitna mere pass hai mere jeevan mein phir bhi pyas hai* (The sea is so close to me, and yet I remain thirsty)."

Lalpur, part of the Amarpur block in Dindori, was predominantly a tribal settlement: the Gond tribe accounted for 112 of the 150 homes that made up the village. Despite the perennial river that flew close to the village, the rain was the only water source for the crops. Although the soil was fertile, the villagers could grow only two crops, namely, maize in the rainy season and mustard (*rai*) in winter, the crops that can come up on the parched land. On average, each household owned about 1 ha but could not produce enough from that piece of land to sustain a family. They worked for wages; most of them earned their living from MGNREGA, a central government scheme that promises paid employment – manual labour – for at least 100 days each year. Most women in he village were active members of functional self-help groups.

"Gaon me nadi behti hai aur hum paani ko taras rahe hain (A river flows across the village, yet we crave water)." These words of the members of one such self-help group were buzzing in my ear. I was thinking, "Despite our intense and long-term efforts, have we development professionals actually been able to meet even the villagers' basic needs? Water scarcity was the root cause of many of the ills that dogged the villagers, whereas we have been working hard to alleviate the symptoms but not the cause. I knew that the ongoing project did not exactly focus on water, but then I also knew that my organisation believed in 'true development' and would support any initiative that would help in achieving that development".

My inner voice started urging me: "Go for it and make sure that all the farms get water throughout the year." I should confess that neither the terrain nor the people of Lalpur were new to me, but the solution had to be unique for both.

I kept thinking, and the search for a solution continued. I vividly remember a discussion on the lift irrigation system and how it had proven useful in Gumla, in Jharkhand, a challenging landscape. After discussing the matter with one of my colleagues, I decided to visit Gumla along with Prashant, my colleague working in Lalpur for two years, and two local community leaders to understand the system and the process.

Once I understood the working of that three-year-old lift

irrigation system and talked to the villagers managing it, I was convinced that this was the solution for Lalpur. However, I decided to keep this to myself.

We then arranged an excursion for some members of Sharda, one of the self-help groups in Lalpur. I had faith in the technology but wanted the community members to realise what they had to do to make it work. After all, technology is not enough: what any development project needs for success is the participation of people who put their heart and soul into the project. While the community members discussed the matter themselves, I set out to find the cost. Even before we left Gumla, I was buoyed by what Premlata, one of the executive members of the Sharda self-help group, said: "*Dekh kar lagta hai hum bhi nadi ke panni ko waadi me la sakte hain. Bus gaon me ekta banani hogi.*" (It seems that we too can bring water from the river to our farms—provided we stand united and work together.) Women excursionists seemed confident. I, however, kept them reminded during the return journey: "If your sisters in Gumla could do it, so could you. And, if you do it, you will be recognised as the angels who brought water to the village and made everyone prosperous. You would also set an example for others."

Prashant, who used to visit Lalpur frequently, informed me that he had overheard the villagers discussing the lift irrigation system. The positive buzz in the village was palpable. The following week, Premlata called a village meeting inviting everyone in the hamlet to discuss solar lift irrigation. It didn't take much time for the entire village to shout in unison: *"Hum bhi karenge, aur achche se karenge* (We will do it, and we will do it better)."* Word of mouth had worked. *Chingari sulag gayi thi* (A spark had struck, and smouldering had started).

I was happy with the outcome, but my happiness proved short-lived. Several questions had to be settled first: Would the technology succeed in this area? Will I be able to mobilise enough funds, amounting to lakhs of rupees? How would the already poverty-stricken community contribute?

After the meeting, I discussed my plan with the rest of my team and my superiors in Pradan. Although I had expected a go-ahead, I never thought it would come so soon and that too without any follow-up questions and apprehensions. Funds are always a critical issue in any development project. Maybe because I presented the case with such passion and confidence, my team and superiors decided to leave the matter of funding to me.

The challenge before me was twofold: finding assured funding and forming a well-knit team to take the task forward. The Sharda self-help group was a functional one, with active leaders forthcoming to the idea of solar lift irrigation. Pooran, the husband of one of the members of Sharda, had been a very vocal supporter ever since his wife had told him about the lift irrigation proposal.

The installation site was going to be crucial to the entire project.

Two other major considerations were the amount of water likely to be available and the maximum number of farms that it would be able to irrigate. I was aware that no one site would be acceptable to all, and each farmer would like it to be closer to his or her farm. Selected village community representatives and I began to walk along the riverbank, searching for the most suitable spot. Pooran stopped at one location to say that it was the most appropriate. Although the water was not too deep there, the site was not centrally located. As no other member supported Pooran, I Looked towards Prashant because he knew the place well. He signalled his dissension and averted his eyes. I intervened and suggested that we explore a few more sites before making a firm choice. After some searching, we found a suitable spot that met our needs. In the evening, while Prashant and I were discussing both the locations with another group of farm owners, primarily women, it turned out that Pooran had insisted on the first location because most of his fields were nearby!

Within a couple of days, in consultation with the villagers and an expert from Syngenta Foundation, our partner in Jharkhand, the second location was finalised.

Based on the location and the number of solar panels, the total cost was estimated at 8.35 lakh rupees. From discussions with my colleagues, it emerged that, with a few donors pitching in and Pradan's contribution, I could raise only about 4 lakh rupees. I wondered what we could expect from the villagers, who barely earned enough to have two square meals a day.

I requested Prashant call an urgent meeting where every household would be represented. Two members of our team were given the task of visiting every family and personally requesting their participation in the meeting. Our efforts paid off, and we had a full house. Almost everyone from the village was present, including children. The meeting started with Prashant informing all the members about the chosen location and how long it would take for the installation to be complete if we started right away. That won resounding applause from the audience. It was my turn next.

"I am happy to inform you that we, with the help of you all, are close to banishing our misery. I know your lands are fertile, and you always give your blood and sweat to the fields, but you don't get enough returns because you cannot irrigate them. Gajanan, the engineer from Syngenta Foundation, estimates the project to cost about 8.35 lakh. Pradan is happy to contribute about half of the total, and you all, the community members whose fields will be irrigated, have to share the rest," I announced.

This was a heart-breaking statistic for the community members, who hardly had any disposable income, and was greeted with stunned silence. I had almost given up hopes when, all of a sudden, Hansi stood up and announced, *"Bhaiya hum sablog jarur koshish karbo. Thoda time de do.*

(Brother, we will try; please give us some time)."

I knew that it was going to be tough, and I needed to look for some other sources of funding, but the words of Hansi did boost my confidence. After all, we needed to invest only once, whereas the prosperity would be forever.

The same night, the leaders of self-help groups held an emergency meeting to discuss the matter. The meeting turned out to be a short one—the participants were unanimous in pledging their full support. They also suggested using the Community Investment Fund provided by MPSRLM (Madhya Pradesh State Rural Livelihood Mission, part of a national mission launched by the Ministry of Rural Development of the Government of India) as a loan. As soon as the meeting ended, I was informed of the decision. To me, the idea seemed plausible. I requested Premlata and Gandiya Bai to announce this decision to the villagers.

The next day, as Prashant and I were discussing the way forward, a group of villagers came to us and said they would like to withdraw from the lift irrigation project. I couldn't understand this overnight change of opinion. But, after some probing, the real reason surfaced when one of the women said, "*Hum sabki zameen ka rakba to alag hai fir sab barabar loan kyun lenge?*" (When our fields are of unequal size, why should the loan amount be the same for all?) The argument made sense. Accordingly, we divided the total cost by the entire land to be irrigated, which worked out to 385 rupees per 'decimal' (a local unit equal to one-hundredth of an acre, or roughly 40 square metres). The villagers happily agreed to the formula *jiski jitni zameen utna hi udhaar aur utna hi wapasi* (The loan and the instalments will be proportional to the land size.) It was further decided that part of the loan could be paid in kind through labour, and the rest could be from the money available with the village organisation. This arrangement convinced the remaining few, mainly those with tiny holdings. To forestall any delay in the availability of funds and loans to the members, I discussed the entire proposal with the district project manager of Dindori MPSRLM, Mr Shyam Gautam. He seemed optimistic about the proposal and assured me that funds would be available to the self-help group on time through their block team. When he wished our team well, I realised that collaboration between institutions works if projects aim at immediate and tangible benefits to the community.

After getting community acceptance for the project, finalising the location, and securing funds, the next major challenge was to lay a 538-metre-long pipeline that met the prescribed technical specifications. Of the total distance, only 90 metres passed through public land; the rest was for the use of individual homesteaders. To ensure that all work was completed in time and conformed to the technical specifications, a few members needed to be selected and trained by the technical experts. We decided to leave the selection to the self-help groups.

It was decided that all would dig the common stretch and that passing through individual homesteads would be dug by the owner of the respective homestead. Also, those who dug the common stretch would be paid wages (or their loans would be reduced accordingly) and the individual members must meet the cost of digging the stretches leading to their fields. The entire work, including laying pipes in privately owned lands, was completed in less than three weeks. I was delighted by the spirit of cooperation and the understanding shown by the community members. Gajanan, who had almost become an honorary consultant for the work, was pleasantly surprised with the quality and the pace of work.

Finally, the momentous day arrived. The villagers seemed excited. Children started gathering at the site. Women, particularly members of the Sharda self-help group, turned up in all their finery. Everybody was waiting for 10.30 a.m., the *subh muhurat* (auspicious moment) at which the lift irrigation scheme was to be inaugurated. Although no formal inaugural function had been planned, some members of the self-help group were busy lining up everyone so that all could witness the first gush of water emerging from the river Kharmer to wet the parched fields of Lalpur.

Excitement mounted as minutes rolled by, the villagers began singing and dancing and then jumped with joy as the cry went up: *"Paani aaye gaish .... paani aaye gaish ... paani aaye gaish ..."* (Water has come... water has come. . . water has come.)

Yes, water was indeed flowing—all the way up to the homesteads. Happiness and hope were written on every face. However, while those whose lands were near the first outlet started using the water, others farther from the source continued to await their turn. Unfortunately, as days passed, disenchantment grew, and some families could not irrigate their fields. Those with easy access to water used it with abandon as the rest waited patiently. The long wait of more than 15 days to receive the promised water was transformed into anger and frustration. Those who had awaited their turn began complaining and threatened to destroy the pipelines already laid.

I realised that equitable and timely water distribution had become a major issue, and I began to grapple with many questions: Will the pipeline, like any other community structure, be usurped by only a few? Will it cease to be relevant to the ordinary people and become another bureaucratic installation in the village? If I don't intervene immediately, will the entire effort and resources go down the drain and, most importantly, my team's and Pradan's credibility be badly dented? Finally, after many sleepless nights, I decided to convene a meeting, talk to the people and sort out the problems related to the operation and maintenance of the system and the distribution of water.

Villagers attending the meeting fell into two distinct groups: those who had used the river water at least once formed one group, and those who were yet to get benefit formed the other. Although everyone was silent, the anger among members of the second group was palpable. I realised that if I allowed members to speak, the only result would be heated arguments, and we would achieve nothing. I decided to accept full responsibility for the present sorry state of affairs.

I began, "first of all, let me once again congratulate all of you, and I am happy to see that your solar lift irrigation system is working well. However, I must accept that we overlooked the issues of equitable distribution and operation and maintenance. Because of this lapse, some members have been getting water all the time, whereas the majority are yet to get even a single drop. This doesn't seem right; everybody has an equal right to the system, and each should get water in proportion to the size of one's holding. We should agree on a suitable mechanism for water distribution in today's meeting—which will continue until we reach an agreement."

Both the groups accepted the agenda. We took a short break for dinner and resumed at 8.30 p.m. I requested members to lay down rules for (1) distribution and equitable sharing of water, (2) operation and maintenance of the lift irrigation system, and (3) charges to be paid by users. It took more than four hours to reach a consensus. The outcome of this meeting was the formation of a water-users group named *Maa Narmada Navjal Sinchai Samiti*, membership criteria, rules for submitting a request for irrigation, members' right to exchange their turn with other members, hourly fee for water usage, norms for running the group, managing funds, and, finally, a mechanism to settle disputes, if any. The meeting ended with the participants singing praises of this newly formed group. Although it was past midnight, I was content with the outcome and hoped that the water would keep flowing uninterrupted forever.

Afterword

It's not even three seasons since the solar-powered lift irrigation system became functional the village had already turned greener. Although the number of beneficiaries was small and the irrigated area was limited, access to water has brought in many unexpected changes. More than 4 hectares of land was being used for growing vegetables such as cauliflower, tomato, spinach, and cowpea, all grown using modern farming methods. Also, all the families have started mango orchards on their homesteads. As a result, the people in the settlement earned up to 40,000 rupees more every year. They started repaying their loans to the village organisation within one year from the income from vegetables grown between rows of the mango plants. Taking inspiration from Lalpur, 18 households from Parsel, another village, came together to set up a similar system covering approximately 12 hectares—and some more had planned to replicate the experience.

Apart from farming, some members of self-help groups used the water for other purposes – brickmaking, for example, as part of another government-run scheme (the prime minister's housing scheme) – and earned a profit. The entire exercise of bringing water from the Kharmer river to the village had made the members and the community itself more confident. Their negotiation power in the local market was greater, and the villagers were respected and talked about. After visiting Parsel, the district collector of Dindori appreciated the model and decided to expand it to other areas within the district.

With the systems in place and operators trained, I was sure the solar lift would continue to lift villagers economically higher and higher.

*****

An Incredible Journey from Barrenness to Salvation

(Kumar Thangavelsamy & Saranmoyee Kar)

"It was like a theatre show when all nine of us women started presenting our watershed plan to Gram Sabha. Many villagers were capturing the moment through their mobiles."

The story begins...

It was the year 2016, and the setting was the impoverished, forest-fringed adjacent tribal villages of Birbandh, Majgerya, and Kharujhor in the Jangalmahal region of Bankura district, West Bengal. The tribal community, which predominantly inhabited the villages, were extremely hard-working yet impoverished. These villages had a combined population of 755, of which the majority were dependent on agriculture and daily-wage labour. Though the situation had improved in the last few years because of assured wages of Rupees 213.00 per day for 100 days in a year under the government-sponsored Mahatma Gandhi National Rural Employment Act (MGNREGA), on the whole, the villagers still remained distressed. They tried every trick, worshipped all their goddesses, and contacted local government officials, but to no avail. The highly unpredictable monsoon and undulated sloping terrains causing high run-off resulted in frequent crop failures. They could cultivate just one crop of paddy a year, with very low productivity.

In 2016, when Professional Assistance for Development Action (hereafter Pradan) started working in the village, Mr Arup was confused and was not sure about where to start. He didn't wish his seniors to know of his dilemma. "When I received a call from the office, after almost a fortnight of my joining, asking about my progress, I gave a vague answer that I had completed the background study and was planning to start a natural resource management-based livelihood intervention", recalled Arup.

The very first thing Arup did was to encourage villagers to change the crop from traditional rice to vegetables. He tried to impress villagers that paddy is more cost and labour-intensive but less remunerative than vegetables. He arranged a two days training for the villagers. During training, the focus remained on the migration from conventional paddy to vegetable cultivation.

Arup's experiences with the villagers gave him the impression that working with the women's group would be more effective. He had observed that the men folk remained more interested in working as daily wagers, by either visiting nearby cities or working in the village under the MGNREGA scheme. Also, he observed that women were more concerned about their family's problems.

"Generally, tribal women are considered more hardworking than their male counterparts. I found a few didis (elder sisters) such as, Aloki, Shefali, Sarathi, Sharmila, Ramani, Rani, Ramani, Ashalata and Gita to be forthcoming, strong-willed, and ready to work for the entire village. A Self-help group (SHG) was formed with these women as its founding members. The membership swelled to 20 within a week, and today there are more than 100 members," Arup informed.

Women leaders of the SHG took the initiative of convincing their families and the rest of the villagers to adopt vegetable cultivation on an experimental basis. Unfortunately, from day one, the male members started ridiculing these women, questioning their knowledge and experience in farming. Few older men even asked who had permitted them to do all these activities. Seeing the men's intense opposition, most villagers, except those nine founding members, decided to stay away from the SHG's works. However, those courageous nine took up the challenge, went against their family members, and invested from their own SHG savings to cultivate tomatoes and beans on trellises, on smaller pieces of their respective lands. They followed all the practices suggested to them during the training.

The first few weeks went as planned, and the courageous nine were happy. However, they couldn't irrigate their crops during the fruiting stages, leading to mortality and pest infestation in the standing crops. The crop wasn't as successful as it was expected. These nine women became the subject of ridicule and derogatory comments. These women were shocked to see the responses of the men and some of their fellow women in the village. They were in awe.

Arup decided to meet them as a group and motivate them again. "I gave them examples from the Ramayana and the Indian freedom struggle. One of my colleagues shared a couple of inspirational stories of tribal women of Jharkhand leading the change from the front. It took some time, but they agreed to take their mission forward," remembered Arup.

The courageous nine visited each house, individually or in groups of three or four, met the elders and requested help. These women leaders were persuasive enough to convince the villagers that they were doing all this to bring the community out of poverty. After they had visited almost 90% of the houses, the SHG organised a meeting of all the villagers. The meeting, attended by nearly everyone in the village, was very successful and historical. The entire community had come together for the first time to discuss a common problem. The meeting, which started in the afternoon, continued till late evening. The men were surprised to note the women's understanding of agriculture practices. My team continued to play the second fiddle to the courageous nine. It was concluded that lack of enough water was the root cause of the village's problems.

"The meeting changed the opinion of the entire village towards these women and their mission", informed Arup.

Sarathi di smiled as she recalled their failure, "The loss that we incurred during our first venture as a group was very hard for us. The men in the village were constantly ridiculing us for our initiative. They taunted us, saying that women would first cultivate tomatoes on trellises, and after a few days, paddy also would be cultivated on trellises, and finally, they would control agriculture. So, when our venture failed, they (men) thought that we would step back. But on the contrary, we went to them and started discussing the cause of our failure. They did not expect this. For us, it was not the end but the beginning of a new journey."

This was the watershed event after which these courageous nine transformed into change agents and started working on natural resource management in the village. Encouraged by their interest and belligerence, Arup decided to provide more field-based exposures to them so that they could see, talk, and learn from village leaders who had done good work for their respective villages.

A team of 20 women, including the courageous nine, toured Bandudih in the Purulia district which had taken steps to conserve its land and water by implementing watershed principles. These touring women were shown and given videos of successful water conservation interventions by the villagers as gifts.

On their return, the women who were part of the exposure visit conducted meetings in various hamlets of all three villages.

They enthusiastically shared their experiences and shared the videos collected during their visits. These women leaders knew how to present facts in front of villagers so that they understood them quickly. For example, to explain "ridge and valley", a scientific approach to water conservation, Sharmila di put it in this way: "So what you do is, it is like a bank; we have to deposit water in the uplands, so that we can withdraw it as and when required, in the lowlands." Most of the villagers understood this example easily.

Unfortunately, meetings in many hamlets didn't go well. In a few hamlets, fellow villagers even booed some of the members who faltered while explaining technical concepts. However, when one member felt down and discouraged, others were there to pull their fellow sisters up.

"Though I have forgotten the name but still remember what we were told by a very old lady. She had told us that we needed to work as a team, just like the five fingers of our hands work. If one of them is injured, the rest of the fingers do their job temporarily. Once the injured finger is alright again, they go back to working together," said Rani di, the youngest among the courageous nine. She enthusiastically continued to share her learning, "We were also told that in every society, the majority would be interested in mocking those who wanted to do something different, even if it was for the good of society. We always remembered these lines."

Arup explained, "My entire team and I felt so proud of these tribal women when we found them actively participating in developing a watershed plan for three villages. Our documentation team and watershed experts had to play the supporting role to these women SHG members."

Arup was right in praising the women leaders of the villages of Birbandh, Kharujhor and Majhgerya, as the development of a common watershed management plan by illiterate women had never been heard of before. External experts had played a crucial role even in the villages these women leaders had visited to see and learn a few weeks earlier.

"When I shared this with my colleagues in one of our monthly meetings, my colleagues told me that they would be touring my village to meet SHG members", informed Arup.

The women leaders sought a meeting of the Gram Sabha to present their plan and seek their approval. These courageous nine rehearsed their presentation a couple of times.

"It was like a theatre show when all nine of us women started presenting our watershed plan. Many villagers were capturing the moment through their mobiles, as it was for the first time that women members were proposing their plan to the entire Gram Sabha. We were being watched as if we were doing something extraordinary. Frankly, I was delighted to see this", narrated excited Ashalata.

Everyone appreciated the plan, including the Gram Panchayat (GP) head and elected members. But to the utter surprise of these women, their plan was not included in the annual action plan of the GP. The courageous nine reached the office of the local Block Development Officer (BDO) and made another presentation in front of the BDO. Unfortunately, the block administration also did not consider it for implementation.

"Even we were surprised to see that their plan was not considered", says Arup.

The combative women leaders continued meeting all the members of the GP and the concerned government officials. In 2017, with the launch of 'Usharmukti' (salvation from barrenness), a Government of West Bengal flagship program, the women saw hope. The entire concept of Usharmukti revolved around the spirit of "Ajker Mojuri, Kalker Jibika (Today's wage, Tomorrow's livelihood)", aimed at rejuvenating the seven rivers of West Bengal, flowing in the western part of West Bengal. The Usharmukti program needed a watershed approach to be successful in the region, and fortunately, the plan prepared by the women leaders of Birbandh, Kharujhor and Majhgerya fitted the bill. It was decided that the women farmers of the village would be a part of the Planning and Monitoring Team of this flagship project, along with the representatives of government agencies and an NGO. The entire team, particularly members from the government departments, was astonished that the women could organise focused group discussions, carry out proper resource mapping, and develop a feasible action plan. The plan had women of all three villages central to all the activities. Within 90 days, all the stakeholders accepted the plan and started the work.

"It was a memorable day for me, and I was able to see and experience the change from apprehension and apathy to hope and faith that was reflected on the smiling faces of villagers", said an emotional Arup.

When asked, "What made these women successful?" Arup replied, "Their strong will, grit, and unity, even if they represented three different villages and four tribes. They remained unmoved by failures and criticism".

Sarathi shared their story, "We also went beyond personal benefits, focused on our problems and looked for sustainable solutions. The Usharmukti project was a golden opportunity for us, and we knew that both government agencies and Pradan were there to help us. We wouldn't have found the answer to our problems if this opportunity had been lost. So, we decided to do our part in the best possible way."

The news of the success of the Usharmukti program's spread quickly. Representatives from panchayat, block, and district administration offices became regular visitors to their villages and the structures they created. The increased water availability for irrigation made them the real heroes of their villages. Most of the villagers shifted to vegetable cultivation, and within two years, more than 50% of the total cultivable land was under vegetable cultivation. Once mono-cropped with paddy, villagers' farms were used for growing brinjal, tomato, cabbage, cauliflower, and chilli. This was achieved with the help of the small water harvesting structures created in the corners of every alternative field. The moisture-retention capacity of the area increased considerably as almost all the uplands in the village were covered with plantations, followed by the excavation of a series of water-harvesting structures. Because of these women, these villages saw the convergence of various projects of different government departments such as sericulture, agriculture, and irrigation. Overall, the transformation was evident in these villages, with fallow uplands converted into lush green fields.

Afterword

Aloki didi elucidated the change, "We have been facing water crises since our childhood. The crises had been so acute that we found it difficult to take a bath every day. There were just a few tube wells for drinking water, which used to give very little water after long hours of pumping. Usharmukti gave us the scope to rejuvenate our fields; and ever since we sisters have taken up the responsibility for its planning and implementation, wherever you go, you will find water."

The entire region has benefited from the actions of these women. People who opposed women in the initial days are now the beneficiaries. The working of panchayat and block functionaries has changed, and now they do not allow any plantation without soil and moisture conservation activities. These women continue to face opposition because of the political aspirations of a few of the villagers. However, they consider these hindrances to be a recognition of their more significant success.

"The dream of a few women has become a reality for all in the region. Usharmukti is not merely a project of salvation from natural barrenness, it is also a story of transformation, action and belligerence," were the final words of proud Arup.

*****

Cropping Creeping Currencies

(Pradeep Kumar Mishra & Raju Kumar)

"Now I can eat what I want and spend how I want – thanks to the creeper vegetables."

The story begins...

For a commoner, the Bastar district symbolises unlawful insurgency. It has been the centre of the Naxal movement and has seen the killings of several senior police officers and political leaders. In addition, Bastar is also the densely forested land of tribes such as, the Maria Gonds, Murias, Halbas, and Dhurwas, who make up one-fourth of Chhattisgarh's tribal population. The geographical landscape of the entire district is picturesque and filled with natural flora and fauna. People are simple and have mostly been insulated from development in the rest of the country.

Pakhnar Dogihirmapara village in the Darbha block of Bastar district was one of those villages which were very far from the district headquarters and had never been on the government's agenda. Most of the villagers lived like aboriginals and depended mainly on forests and forest products for survival. A single-room hut housed four to five members of a family, who relied on foodgrains made available through a government-run public distribution system (PDS). Unfortunately, they could barely manage to have two square meals a day. Most of the families owned arable lands. The average landholding of the households in the block was more than three acres, and the area received about 1450 mm of average annual rainfall. What a paradox! Owners of fertile land in a resource-rich area were living in abject poverty!

"*Atisundar*! (very beautiful)" was the first word Mr Raju, a young professional from Pradan, uttered after reaching the village. Though his seniors told him that he needed to work hard and be careful, he seemed lost in the place's natural beauty.

"Sir, I have walked for a few kilometres to reach this place. I have been told that you have come here to help the poor," revealed Hidme, a woman from Pakhnar Dogihirmapara village. After talking with her for a few minutes, Raju realised that the area needed urgent interventions before the natives experienced dire hunger and took to arms, thereby turning insurgent. He studied the village profile to find that more than 50% of the children below five years were underweight, and about 70 per cent of the women of reproductive age suffered from anaemia. Only one-third of their total income came from agriculture, even if most were landowners. They mainly cultivated paddy, of which the productivity was too low. Although they grew a few vegetables, these were meant only for self-consumption, and no serious effort was made to obtain a better harvest. Women of the area collected tendu patta, tamarind, and other non-timber forest products. At times, they worked as daily-wage labourers and sold homemade liquor in the local markets. Raju quickly concluded that the situation was precarious and urgent action was needed.

It was not difficult to recommend cultivating high-value crops, but Raju knew that the tribals of Darbha neither had the awareness nor the skills to do so. Also, changing cropping patterns would require changing their generations-old traditional thinking and routine lifestyles. Raju knew that these changes were not going to be easy. With no other option in sight, Raju decided to contact his team and have discussions with them before taking action.

Raju decided to have an initial meeting with all the villagers. He was still new to the villagers, so he decided to visit Hidme. Hidme was pleasantly surprised to find Raju in the village. Excited, Hidme started introducing him to her husband and other neighbours without wasting much time. Raju was surprised to see that although Hindi was not the native language of the villagers, they could understand and express themselves in Hindi.

After introducing himself as a local Chhattisgarhi, he told them, "I have come here to seek your help in helping all of you to earn more so that all can eat and live with dignity." Raju was expecting some response from the villagers. Unfortunately, no one responded, though there were murmurs.

After a silence of about a minute, Raju asked Hidme – "Do you or your fellow villagers have any doubts or queries?"

Hidme looked around and stood up after her husband signalled her to speak. She told Raju, "It is good that you have come to our village and talked to us. We are poor people and have nothing to share. But if you tell us what to do, we would be happy to join you."

After listening to Hidme, Raju decided to make himself very clear. He asked them, "Will you all help me, if I request you to do something that will give you more money, not just for a day but month after month?"

There was an instant answer from one of the young women, "Bhaiya, we live in the forest, this has been our home for generations, and it will continue to be so. So, we will not co-operate with you if you want to suggest anything that will harm our forests."

"*Didi*, why do you say so? I haven't suggested anything", was Raju's counter-question. Though Raju knew he was slightly deviating from his planned message, he decided to indulge the lady in keeping the interaction alive.

However, instead of the young lady, Hidme replied, "We keep getting requests to cut trees or hunt animals for money, but we have not accepted those, and shall never do so."

Raju was surprised and returned to his original subject. "No, you will not do anything with forests; you will do something you have been doing around the year in your backyard", replied Raju. Almost the entire village nodded in agreement.

"Day after tomorrow at 10.00 a.m. , all adults are invited for a meeting. We will learn how to make money. And, join me for lunch too", was the concluding remark cum invitation of Raju. The villagers appeared happy and surrounded Hidme asking her many questions. Raju returned home, thinking of his next course of action, as he was sure of participation from at least 50% of the households during the proposed meeting.

Raju and his team were ready for the meeting. More than a hundred chairs were placed under a colourful tent. There was a small dais with five chairs on it. It was not even 9.00 a.m. when the villagers started arriving at the venue. Raju was happy to see the villagers coming early.

Most of them were well-dressed. All the seats were occupied, but the villagers continued pouring in. Raju requested his colleagues for an additional carpet. When Raju and the guests reached the dais, the venue was jam-packed. Everyone was waiting for the meeting to start, as they were interested in learning how to earn money.

Before the meeting started, Raju invited the two oldest villagers, Mr Gundana and Mrs Sinduriya and offered seats on the dais. The villagers were happy. Raju began his speech by talking about the fertile soil, availability of ample water, and the hard-working people of the area and acknowledging their contribution to preserving the surrounding forests. It was probably the first time for the villagers that somebody was praising them and their village. They welcomed it with applause. However, there was complete silence as soon as Raju asked about their financial status.

He used silence to emphasise his next point, "*Na madeera na jungle, ab hoga bagwaani se mangal*" (Neither wine nor forest, there will be happiness because of horticulture). Though there was another round of applause by a few villagers, most started looking at each other to understand what it meant. Raju proposed his plan for the villagers to consider. Later, an agriculture scientist and local agriculture officers also explained the process and benefits of horticulture. During lunch, Raju and the visitors remained surrounded by the villagers. The process and income from project *Bagwaani* remained central to all their talks. While male members were seen discussing investment versus returns, women villagers wanted to know more about the next step of the *Bagwaani* project.

There were two half-day demonstration training for the villagers over the next two weeks. Raju and his team realised that women members were more interested and seemed serious about cultivating vegetables. The focus was on growing creepers that carried vegetables such as beans, tomato, bottle gourd, bitter gourd, and pumpkin. These plants are primarily climbers, which need the support of a pole of a tree to grow.

Scientists were surprised to see Raju's more profound understanding of the needs and limitations of women villagers. Raju had requested that they suggest those crops that need smaller space, can be grown quickly even on backyard farms, don't require many resources, are part of villagers' existing food habits, and are more nutritious. The decision to focus on creeper vegetables was unanimously taken by the Pradan team, scientists, and officers of the agriculture department. "I was delighted to see that women members readily agreed to grow these crops and join the project we had planned for them," recalls Raju.

Impressed with the project and encouraged by the training, Hidme discussed her plan of vegetable cultivation with her husband. Not convinced about its success, her husband discouraged her and advised her against it. But Hidme decided to work alone. She took a loan from the SHG and started working. Within just 90 days Hidme's husband saw the fruits of her hard work and persistence, and began assisting her with the farming. He helped her by selling the vegetables in the local market. He was now sure of the benefits of vegetable cultivation. He fenced the homestead land to increase the area under cultivation. As suggested by the scientists, the use of trellises proved very effective. For the first time, the family had disposable income. Hidme cultivated creepers, particularly bitter gourd, using the trellis and pit method on a plot smaller than 0.1 acres. She earned about 30000 rupees by selling vegetables and repaid the entire loan taken from the SHG.

"Now I can eat what I want and spend how I want – thanks to the creeper vegetables," were the words of a happy Hidme.

Hidme's success motivated a few more women in the village. They found a new method of vegetable cultivation, which was less cumbersome and demanded less drudgery. Within a year, more than 22 farming families from the village got involved in creeper vegetable cultivation. Raju's efforts to extend this practice to the neighbouring village met with some initial resistance. Demonstrations on a few plots did convince farmers, but specially tailored training did not yield the desired results.

"We had to develop pictorial and audio-visual training aids to match the villagers' understanding and language, "said Raju. A Farmer's Field School (FFS) was established in one of the villages to further strengthen the training and capacity building process. Since 2018, more than 900 farmer-training events have been organised by FFS.

Now the creeper movement had spread to two villages. More and more farmers were getting interested in using the *Bagwaani* to improve their economic status. Women were more enthusiastic about the project as it allowed them to decide about the crops and their cultivation. In addition, this also earned them much-needed social status. More families became interested, and existing farmers, who were increasing their cultivation areas, added to the unprecedented demand for quality seeds. Raju knew that ensuring on-time quality inputs at farmers' doorsteps was difficult. For the traders, it was not economical to come down to the village regularly with smaller supplies. Raju and the team now mooted the idea of promoting Agri-entrepreneurs (AEs) amongst the villagers.

For Raju and his team, things were getting easier. Women SHG federations identified five experienced community trainers as AEs. Team Pradan hand-held these trainers to start their respective ventures. Village organisations provided the initial capital as a loan from their Community Investment Fund, a grant received under the National Rural Livelihood Mission (NRLM). Three AEs learnt the business tricks swiftly and started delivering seeds and other inputs to the farmers' doorsteps. Besides providing input supplies, they also picked up produce from the farm gates for marketing. Vegetables from this new band of farmers were fetching reasonable prices as these were considered to be locally-grown and organic.

The farmers of the Dhabra block continued farming traditionally and did not use agrochemicals. Finding the yield lower for most farmers, Raju and his team started promoting standard organic farming practices. For this, Raju invited one of his colleagues from a nearby district who helped introduce the techniques of compost pits, vermicomposting, and NADEP (National Agribusiness Development Program) tanks on the homestead lands. *"Ek khodra, Ek tagadi"* (One pit, One pan) was the slogan adopted to ensure the optimal application of these techniques.

Women farmers were now ready to accept any advice from the team Pradan. Moreover, they found it simpler and cheaper. Later on, at the FFS, farmers learned the application and efficacy of bio-pesticides in controlling diseases and pest attacks. Growing vegetables had become cost-effective. Many families joined the bandwagon of creeper-vegetable cultivators. Production was rising, and farmers started having a considerable market surplus. All these changes came about in just 18 months. Hidme and her fellow villagers were happy, and so was Raju.

"After I found that our creeper project had started growing, I scouted for bigger markets for our organic products. I knew that negotiating with the bulk buyers and ensuring a regular, timely supply of fresh vegetables of the required quantity was tough for these individual farmers. So, I decided to institutionalise the process and make it easier for common farmers", says Raju.

As the total number of farmers had swollen to more than 1000, villages were divided into clusters. The farmers of a given cluster brought their produce to a designated place on a selected day. The AE responsible for the given cluster carried out the vegetables' aggregation, weighing, sorting, grading, and packaging. After deducting the commission, farmers were paid for their produce at a pre-determined price. As a result, Darbha's organic vegetables started getting sold in the markets of bigger towns like Jagdalpur, Raipur, and Dantewada. A Cluster-level Federation monitored the whole process, which was termed Micro-production Arrangements (MPA). The success of MPA provided the platform for forming a Farmers Producers Organisation (FPO). The idea behind the FPOs was to provide farmers with formal business identity and let them manage various activities by themselves.

Villagers could earn and save money; however, they were still hesitant to make big investments such as water pumps, farming larger areas, and growing crops that required high investments. However, regular meetings with the farmers and the interventions' positive impact helped mobilise them, and villagers slowly started loosening their purses for investment. Further, this experiment with vegetable cultivation as a source of sustainable livelihood was successful. Government agencies that had been hitherto sceptical in putting their money came forward and started investing in supporting villagers' collective actions for an alternative source of income.

Raju remembers, "Yes, the outsiders did say that we were doing everything for the community and were anxious about what would happen when I left the place. I told them to visit those villages and see who took the farming decisions, sold the inputs, managed the procurement for despatch, and decided upon the financial transactions. They would find that the villagers only carried out all these activities."

To all those who repeatedly question the future potential of the villagers, Raju has only one answer, "No one has seen the future, but everyone has seen the past. Just see the difference between where were they before the creepers came into their lives and where are they today... Never, ever undermine the abilities of the villagers."

Afterword

"Today, this model is being talked about throughout the state. Every alternate week, you will find that some team or the other comes to meet uneducated, poor villagers turned rich entrepreneurs. We are in the third year of intervention, and about

5000 women farmers of 54 villages of Darbha block are part of our mission," says Raju. He adds, "Several families are today able to make an additional income of Rupees 15000 to Rupees 20000 within three months. When we started creeper cultivation in two villages during 2016-17, the total production was 8.0 metric tonnes, which has increased to about 600 metric tonnes by 2020-21."

Raju is satisfied that women like Hidme are happy today. Hidme's husband supports and respects her more than ever before. Villagers remember her as a leader and path breaker. A woman, who had never cultivated vegetables before, has become an 'inspiration and role model' for many women. But for Raju, the journey continues. He still has several villages on his radar; he seems determined to change the lives of many more villagers, just as he did with Hidme and hundreds of women farmers of the village of Pakhnar Dogihirmapara.

*****

Be the Changemaker

(Niraj Kumar)

Page 175

POSTSCRIPT

We have narrated these stories to emphasise that being a true changemaker is a task neither too bookish nor utopian. These stories of success and change seem simple and attainable—they are not stories of alumni of the most respected temples of education in the world or of veterans with established credentials but of those commoners-turned-heroes who seem to have done nothing extraordinary or revolutionary to usher in changes. However, the outcome and the impact of their work are remarkable and proved life-changing for hundreds of poor and distressed souls. But for the insights, prudence, and thoughtful decisions and actions of the protagonists, the suffering communities would have continued to suffer, and the deterioration and depletion of natural resources on which they depend continued unabated.

Each story had its own context and problems. The communities had different levels of appreciation of their problems and readiness to solve them. What is noteworthy is that in some of the cases, the communities had tried on their own to address their concerns but had failed. In some instances, the causes of the problems were natural, such as unfertile lands and irregular rainfall, and beyond the community's control; in others, the causes lay in the people themselves—the result of ignorance, apathetic local institutions, and corruption. Many of the villages were not on the radar of government agencies, and even when they were, development was yet to reach them. However, when invited, cajoled, explained to, and convinced, the government agencies proved very useful in bringing about desirable changes in the villages.

It is appropriate to mention here, and to caution readers, that the book features only success stories and ignores failures: the reality is that neither all endeavours to bring about change are successful nor all successful endeavours, although praiseworthy, are exemplary. Secondly, these stories do not explain the rural realities that can be considered all-encompassing and complete. The realities may even be simpler but equally may be far more complex and incomprehensible. Next, the stories do not imply that heroes and changemakers are preconditions for transformation. It is also possible that the process of change initiated by the community identifies and produces changemakers. For the changemakers, Bharat, the Indian hinterland, is a unique mosaic of diversity and offers possibilities and opportunities in different shades.

The following sections follow a simple formula, although not exhaustive and all-inclusive, which emerged from the stories and, if followed, will make you resilient and your journey as a changemaker smoother and more engaging. Rest assured that the results will be phenomenal, and you will be a hero.

Convince: changes are for the better

In most cases, the symptoms and the causes were apparent, and the community had been experiencing their ill effects for a long time. In general, communities are believed to be resistant and hesitant to change, but the stories tell us that it is not always true. If the problem's severity is conveyed well or felt acutely by the community, changes could be faster and smoother. In the initial days of intervention, community responses were never overwhelming and absolute. Some people did not accept the interventions because they believed that the interventions would change the existing social norms or because experience had made them sceptical of success.

Women: the better half

Most of the stories show that women can lead. Women were more active, and most stories are about their struggles, better livelihoods, and self-esteem. Pradan, the organisation whose stories have been selected deliberately, also focuses more on women. The members of this organisation believe that working with women has a holistic and more sustainable impact. Also, the SHGs have made women more enterprising and vocal, ready to take the lead and work for the community regardless of their socio-economic status. The stories suggest that women, although socially marginalised, suppressed, and deprived of some of their natural rights, did not let go of any opportunity to speak up and fight for their rights.

Want them to be with you? Become one of them

Most of the professionals were not of the native soil; yet, they became community heroes, unsung by outsiders but celebrated by locals. Was their success due to their training and empathetic thinking? Their grounded upbringing or honesty and dedication to their profession? Was it because their hearts bled for the poor and the marginalised? The answer is that their success was due to all of the above. These heroes were the changemakers, and almost all of them would eventually leave for a new place once they believed that the community leadership was empowered enough to take the work forward or because their organisation thought they were more needed elsewhere. What made them heroes was their ability to immerse themselves in the local milieu, appreciate and feel the needs of the community, win people's confidence, engage the community in dialogue, diagnose the real problem, scout for and select the most feasible solution, let the community take ownership, and encourage, guide, and give credit to the village leadership.

Communicate to assure and persuade

Approaching and communicating with the community proved crucial to the success of most interventions. Respect, fairmindedness, harmonising everyone's view before making a decision, and using multiple channels to influence were found to have traction with the communities. Taking opinion leaders into confidence before talking to the communities helped the professionals-turned-heroes to reach community members quickly and effectively. Demonstrations, excursions, and field trips convinced the local leaders of the technologies and helped them learn community-based management systems. The personal credibility of the professionals helped them reach out to the community and get frank feedback.

Simple innovations are magical

Innovative ideas and concepts remained the crux of the success of the local heroes. Whether it was the power of solar energy, creeping creepers, or the concept of 'chasi bandhu', every professional used unique but simple, effective, and inexpensive ideas to bring about change. Innovative ideas have the advantage of being novel, feasible, and beneficial.

Funds, education, and sophisticated laboratories are not necessarily the prerequisites to successful innovation. Anyone – you, your colleagues, or any of your naïve villagers – can be an innovator.

Follow to lead

Who made the final decisions affecting stakeholder participation and project implementation? The villagers did try to use their skills with little or negligible success. Yes, it was the professionals' responsibility to search for all possible options, evaluate their feasibility in the given context, and share it with the villagers; however, the professionals left the final decision to the local community and its leaders. Villagers were educated using audio-visual aids, excursions and field trips, demonstrations, and personal counselling by experts and professionals. Finally, it was the villagers who decided to adopt a technology or a suggestion once they were convinced that it was their best option.

Finding new ones is good; managing existing ones is better

Resource mobilisation is one of the most critical activities for any development professional. It is clear from the stories that the professionals worked to meet the community's needs and did not allow themselves to be constrained by available resources. This approach, although ideal, is challenging to follow. Approaching all possible agencies for the required funds, facilitating the convergence of different government-run programmes, and using villagers' personal and common resources ensured that funds did not hold up community-led and community-oriented works. Mobilising funds and other resources was possible mainly because of the credibility of the professionals, the performance (other agencies were approached only after a piece of work had been completed), and the confluence of the larger objectives shared by all the agencies. The continued focus of the professionals on convergence helped them reap the benefits of synergy among the various agencies, notably different government departments. The professionals knew that government agencies would welcome any move that offers them a credible platform to launch and implement their programmes. Backed with institutional credibility, the professionals approached all such agencies and offered to share the credit for success in return for collaboration and help.

Go for community-led, community-oriented projects

The principle of community-led and community-oriented work helped the changemakers to elicit full and active participation from every member of the community. The leaders of the change ensured that villagers, who were the major stakeholders, remained at the forefront at every stage of intervention, all the way from the beginning to benefit-sharing. As explained above, women took the lead in most cases. As the stories illustrate, SHGs were the most effective means of implementing various activities. In a few selected cases, the members took a tough stand against social discrimination. However, these leaders and members knew that they had full institutional backing of Pradan. Cross-learning among various interventions of Pradan and replicating the successful model in different places were important reasons for their success. At no time did any professional feel helpless or bereft of ideas, because the organization was a treasure trove of experience relevant to bringing about desirable changes in many and varied contexts.

Never lose hope

Not every intervention or effort was successful: a few failed, a few were partial successes, and a few gave the desired results. However, the true development professionals did not despair. Some in their own organisation and many among the community were indifferent; however, as the stories show, these heroes believed in making yet another attempt using different strategies, and ultimately they succeeded. Faith and determined efforts changed age-old traditions, turned barren lands into fertile fields, and brought dejected and oppressed women back into the social mainstream.

I am sure these stories will encourage everyone, young or not so young; every professional, amateur or trained; and every individual, sure or not so sure of success, to join the bandwagon of unknown changemakers who are toiling under trying circumstances to transform the lives of millions for the better. Who knows, many of you who decide to take the plunge today may become the heroes of tomorrow! Who knows, you and any of these unsung heroes may become celebrated and respected leaders in years to come! Don't wait: take the plunge; throw yourself into the battle, and become a changemaker to script yet another incredible story.

*****

About the Authors:

Amit Kumar Singh: Amit, an agricultural engineer, associated with Pradan for the last 17 years. He is also a member of the worldwide network of women's land rights professionals and a fellow WLRVP Program 2014, LANDESA, USA.

Arpan Oraon: Arpan is a B.Tech from NIT Jamshedpur. Currently, with Pradan, he has nine years of experience in the development sector. He works with the most marginalised communities of rural Jharkhand.

Balram Bhushan: Prof. Balram, a Post-Graduation from IIT Bombay and a doctorate from XLRI Jamshedpur, is an academician with twelve years of teaching and research experience. Currently, he is a faculty at the School of Rural Management, XIM University, Bhubaneswar.

Gautam Prateek: Gautam Prateek, MBA from XIMB and doctorate from Arizona State University, USA, is a faculty at the School of Rural Management, XIM University, Bhubaneswar. He has research interests in collective action around the governance of natural resources and rural livelihoods.

Indirah Indibara: Dr Indirah is an assistant professor at the Indian Institute of Management, Raipur with twelve years of teaching and corporate experience. She is an MBA from IIM Kozhikode, a doctorate from XLRI Jamshedpur and has published in journals of international repute.

Jyoti Rekha Roy Pradhan: Jyoti has fourteen years of experience in the development sector. Currently, with Pradan, she is working with a group of federations to help them link with various other feminist networks.

Kumar Thangavelsamy: Kumar Thangavelsamy is an associate professor at the School of Rural Management of XIM University, Bhubaneswar. He has done his B.E from NIT Trichy, masters from MKU, and PhD from IRMA. His academic interests lie in management information systems, data analytics, and digital governance.

Mohini Saha: Mohini, a postgraduate from the IIFM, Bhopal, is a development practitioner associated with Pradan and is based in Chhattisgarh, a tribal dominant state of the country. She has experience working in integrated natural resource management, sustainable livelihood promotion, and nutrition and health.

Niraj Kumar: Prof. Niraj is a faculty of Rural Management at XIM University, Bhubaneswar. An alumnus of GBPUAT Pantnagar, he is a doctorate from IVRI Izatnagar. He has been in academics for more than 25 years.

Pradeep Kumar Mishra: Dr Mishra has more than two decades of experience in academia, industry, and development. He has a doctorate from IRMA, Anand. He teaches finance and general management-related subjects.

Raju Kumar: Raju has a rich experience of more than ten years in the development sector. After completing his MBA, he found his calling in working for the rural community. He is currently working with Pradan in remote tribal belts of Bastar, Chhatisgarh.

Saheb Bhattacharyya: Working with Pradan for the last 17 years, Saheb is currently the team lead of projects in Madhya Pradesh. He has extensively worked in different districts of Jharkhand on watershed development and agro-horticulture model establishment.

Sailabala Panda: Sailabala Panda is a B. Tech from Orissa University of Agriculture & Technology, Bhubaneswar. She is a gender auditor in Pradan and is currently leading land rights works in Pradan across states.

Saranmoyee Kar: Saranmoyee is a postgraduate in social work from Delhi University. She has been working with Pradan since 2015 and has expertise in promoting and nurturing community-based organisations for poor women and nutrition-sensitive agriculture.

Sasanka Sekhar Sahoo: Mr Sahoo is an MBA and has worked in Pradan for the last 12 years. He has worked in different parts of Jharkhand and Odisha and has played a key role in implementing the APC project. Presently, he is the Team Coordinator of Pradan and is located in Keonjhar, Odisha.

Satyendra Nath Mishra: Prof. Mishra is a faculty at the School of Rural Management, XIM University, Bhubaneswar. He is an alumnus of the IRMA, IIFM, Bhopal and TERI School of Advanced Studies, New Delhi.

Shibam Jha: Shibam is an engineer from WBUT. As a development practitioner, he has been associated with Pradan for the past seven years. He has extensively worked in the tribal areas of Chhattisgarh and West Bengal.

Sourav Maity: Sourav is a food technology graduate from Techno India College, Kolkata. He has been working with Pradan for 11 years. An expert in stakeholder mobilisation and large-scale asset creation, he has successfully groomed over 100 women to take leadership positions in village, district and state-level institutions.